I Know the Plans
I Have for You

All Saints Anglican Church, 2003-2023

Copyright ©2024 by Judy Rose

All rights reserved. No part of this book may be reproduced or utilized in any form or by any means, electronic or mechanical, including photocopy, recording, or by an information storage and retrieval system, without permission in writing from the publisher.

ISBN: 979-8-9896268-3-0

Printed and bound in the United States of America
by Ingram Lightning Source

Edited by: Jacque Hillman, Kim T. Stewart, Katie Gould
Layout and design by: Kim T. Stewart
Cover design by: Jacque Hillman, Kim T. Stewart, Wanda Stanfill

The HillHelen Group LLC
470 North Parkway, Suite C
Jackson, TN 38305

The HillHelen Group LLC
635 North 65th Place
Mesa, AZ 85205

(731) 394-2894
www.hillhelengrouppublishers.com
hillhelengroup@gmail.com

I Know the Plans
I Have for You

All Saints Anglican Church, 2003-2023

By Judy Rose

Praise for *I Know the Plans I Have for You*

"What I know to be true about the author of this book is that Judy Rose is a strong believer in Christ. She refuses to compromise her faith in God and His holy Word. I also know that Judy truly strives to be the hands and feet of Jesus, lovingly ministering the love of God to others in need.

"What I didn't know about Judy was her ability to write such an engaging and insightful history of her beloved All Saints Anglican Church. It's obvious how well she has researched her subject and how much she loves the people of whom she writes.

"This is a story about an amazing journey of faith taken by a small group of uncompromising Christians. Their journey has now become a legacy of faith to be cherished. So worth the read!"

—*Christine Veteto, clinic director of Birth Choice, Jackson, Tennessee*

"I am convinced that apart from God and the work of the Holy Spirit, All Saints Anglican Church would not exist.

"Judy Rose has taken powerful testimonies as well as her own personal experience as a charter member and written an inspiring book about our omnipotent God's guidance in planting this great church. This book is a reminder to all of us that God will act and lead when we choose to follow Him!"

—*Melinda Stewart, director of Women's Ministry, Englewood Baptist Church, Jackson, Tennessee*

Dedication

This book is dedicated to the glory of God
and to all the saints who,
in obedience to the one true God,
stepped out in faith those many years ago
to take a stand for the truth.

"'For I know the plans I have for you,'
declares the Lord,
'plans to prosper you and not to harm you,
plans to give you hope and a future.'"
—Jeremiah 29:11, NIV

Table of Contents

Preface	xv
Foreword	xvii
Acknowledgments	xix
Part One: Choose This Day Whom You Will Serve	1
Chapter One: Storm Clouds Gathering	3
The Tornado	3
The Meetings	4
General Convention	4
Bishop Johnson's Visit	6
A Place to Stand Conference, October 2003	7
St. Luke's Vestry Meeting	10
Chapter Two: Sheep without a Shepherd	13
At the Townsends' Home	13
At the Old English Inn	16
At the Warmbrods' Home	18
Looking toward the Future	18
Part Two: Let Goods and Kindred Go	23
Chapter Three: Seek and Ye Shall Find	25
Finding Our Bishop	25
Finding Our Building	31
Finding Our Priest	34
Chapter Four: The Lord Works in Mysterious Ways	39
The Underground Church	39

Chapter Five: Our Kenyan Connection — 45
Visits from Kenya to All Saints — 45
Visits from All Saints to Kenya — 47

Chapter Six: The Move — 49
Adjusting to Our New Home — 49
Making Changes — 54

Part Three: The Lord Will Guide Your Feet — 57

Chapter Seven: Decently and in Order — 59
Our Board — 59
Our First Vestry — 59
Who We Are — 61
Naming the *Crown* — 63
Fellowship — 64

Chapter Eight: Disciples for Christ — 67
Empowered by the Holy Spirit — 67
Small Groups — 68
Children's Ministries — 69
Youth Ministries — 70
Adult Christian Formation — 73
Pastorates — 73
Stewardship — 73
Outreach/Serving Others — 75
Honduras Mission — 77
Other Outreach Ministries — 78

Chapter Nine: Caring for Our Church Family — 81
Serving Our Own People — 81
Pastoral Care — 81
Morning Prayer — 82
Critical Prayer Team — 82

Healing Prayer and Blessing Ministry	82
Silent Retreats	85
Ladies Koinonia	85
Sunday Ministries	86
Fellowship/Hospitality Ministry	86
Music Ministry	86
Altar Guild	92
Flower Guild	93
New Members	94
Lectors	94
Chapter Ten: Rejoice in the Lord Always	**95**
Milestones and Changes	95
In Times of Celebration	96
All Saints' "Firsts"	96
A New Diocese and a New Bishop	96
A New Rector	99
Fifteenth Anniversary Celebration	104
In Times of Adversity	104
Our "Flood"	104
Choir Disharmony	106
COVID	107
More Water Damage	107
Part Four: Hope and a Future	**109**
Chapter Eleven: Mission Abbey	**111**
How It Began	111
The Impact of COVID	114
Breaking Ground	115
Construction Accident	116
Chapter Twelve: Mission St. James	**119**
It Was There All Along	119
A Brief History	119

Chapter Thirteen: Equipping for Ministry	121
Ordained Ministry	121
Serving Our Community	124
All Saints Immigration Services	124
Grief Share	125
Precept Bible Study	125
Chapter Fourteen: To Everything There Is a Season	127
A New Diocese and a New Bishop	127
Bishop Atwood's June 2023 Visit	129
Leaving Our Old Building	131
Fr. Chuck's Sermon: Blessed Is the Path Less Traveled	132
Delays	139
Moving into Our New Building	139
"God's Truth Abideth Still; His Kingdom Is Forever"	143
Notes	145
Appendix	155
1. Founding Members of All Saints	155
2. All Saints Stewards/Board of Directors	156
3. Initial Ministry Chairs	156
4. All Saints Music Directors	156
5. All Saints Clergy	157
6. All Saints First Vestry and Ministry Chairs	158
7. Gifts to All Saints	159
About the Author	164

PREFACE

Every people has a history, a unique story to tell, and All Saints Anglican Church is certainly no exception. Scripture repeatedly commands God's people to remember His wondrous works on their behalf, from Creation to the Exodus to Christ's sacrifice. In I Chronicles, we read that we are to "remember the wondrous works He has done, His miracles and the judgments He uttered." And Joel 1:3 reminds us, "Tell your children of it, and let your children tell their children, and their children to another generation." This book is an effort to help all of us at All Saints remember our remarkable history and all that God has done for us—how we came to be, how God has blessed us along the way, and how He continues to bless us today.

When Jeff Garrety first came to me about twelve years ago with the suggestion that I should write a history of All Saints, enlisting the collaboration of Linda Hayes and Charles Richards, my first reaction was feeling honored that he would ask me to do this. My second reaction was a feeling that I would not be able to undertake such a daunting task. I had never before written a book, and the prospect was somewhat intimidating. At the same time, though, there was a feeling of excitement at being able to share the wonderful story of All Saints' first twenty years.

The idea stayed with me and at times prodded me that I needed to get on with it, but it wasn't until the spring of 2022 that I felt a strong urging from the Holy Spirit that I should do this. I awoke one morning to a clear message, like a text message alert to my brain, about what the first several chapter headings of the book should be. I had not even thought about the book recently, so this really got my attention. I have learned that it is never good to ignore the Holy Spirit, and so it began.

FOREWORD

When, at Jeff Garrety's urging, Judy Rose, Charles Richards, and I first met to consider the codifying of the history of All Saints Anglican Church, the project seemed at once exhilarating and daunting. Our enthusiasm never waned as we brainstormed over several weeks. In less time than we might have hoped, certain ideas as to content, form, style, and purpose solidified.

First, we wanted a faithful rendering of the facts, drawing from firsthand personal memories as well as archived documents. In addition, we envisioned a conversational tone rather than purely expository rhetoric. Finally, we hoped to show the Lord's sovereign will at work throughout our twenty-year history.

Remarkably, Judy has written that book. Indeed, it was evident early on that the Lord had given her the heart to write it and had inspired much of the tone and style we desired. Her writing and research skills and perseverance over countless hours produced the remaining content, meticulously composed and cited.

May the result of her dedication serve to remind us of our miraculous founding and joyous present and may it inform and inspire all those who follow. To God alone be the glory.

—Linda Martindale Hayes
Jackson, Tennessee
March 2024

ACKNOWLEDGMENTS

This book is not a solo endeavor. I would not have been able to write any of this history without the generous help of many people. I contacted many charter members of All Saints, some by email and others in person. Some had moved away, and some had died, but every effort was made to search out those for whom I could find contact information. I am grateful for those who were willing to share their experiences with me. I also sought input from others who came later to All Saints, but who had knowledge about specific events in our history. I have endeavored to present accurate and complete information.

Following in alphabetical order are those people who were most instrumental in helping put this all together.

Fr. Chuck Filiatreau graciously gave his consent for me to use the sermon he gave at All Saints on our last Sunday in the old nave and provided a written copy. He also encouraged me and shared details about our early days.

Gretchen Filiatreau provided a written account of her memories of All Saints' early years. She had a unique perspective that adds much to the background information about how All Saints came to be. I have quoted her frequently, and the entirety of Chapter 4 details her memories of what it was like being on the outside looking in. She has been very supportive of this project.

Joanie Forbes also provided written accounts of her time with us before, during, and after the founding of All Saints. Although she was with us for only four years, she was instrumental (no pun intended) in getting our music ministry up and going and in setting the standard for real Anglican music.

Jane Garrety read the rough draft to check for accuracy. As a member of the original Board of All Saints, she gave valuable input. She also offered advice for ways to improve the text.

As mentioned earlier, Jeff Garrety gave me the idea to write this history and reminded me from time to time that I needed to make a decision about whether or not to accept the challenge. He provided many, many documents and shared his firsthand accounts of major events in our history through conversations and his personal journals and notes. I relied on his advice and wisdom. He also read through the rough draft and offered suggestions and made corrections.

Fr. Wes Gristy shared information about his coming to All Saints, provided a copy of his and Abbie's thoughts on Anglicanism, and pointed me to a trunk full of All Saints memorabilia, including most of the pictures I have used in this book.

Linda Hayes, a dear friend and confidant, has been my number one cheerleader. She has encouraged me, offered suggestions and moral support, and prayed for this project since its beginning. We, along with Charles Richards, met several times in her home where we discussed the book at length and decided what should be included. Her background in journalism and English made her the perfect person to edit the final product.

Fr. Bob Hudson, another member of our original Board of Directors, sent several emails that provided much insight into our early history and offered online sources that contained many documents I have cited. He has been patient in answering the many questions I have asked over the last two years. I appreciate his friendship and his wisdom.

Kathy (Herriman) Trawick left many notes and documents that helped me tremendously in recalling the early milestones and other events in our history. Kathy had been planning to write All Saints' history herself until she moved to Memphis in 2005 and no longer attended All Saints. Even though she didn't write this history, indirectly she had a great influence on the text.

There are others who provided pertinent information for

this book: Terry Blakley, Bev Carr, Marty Courcelle, Joe Davis, Becky Googe, Taylor Laird, Denise Matthews, Dr. Gary Osborne, Malcolm Pearson, Melinda Pearson, Celeste Pope, Stacy Preston, Joanna Priester, Barbara Reed, Charles Richards, Anne Rushing, Dr. Jordan Tang, Lloyd and Lynn Tatum, Walter Townsend, Dr. Jim Warmbrod, and Carrie Whaley.

In publishing this final product, I am grateful to the editors at HillHelen Group Publishers.

And last but not least, I thank the Vestry of All Saints Anglican Church for making a copy of this book available to each All Saints household.

PART ONE:
Choose This Day Whom You Will Serve

"Choose for yourselves this day
whom you will serve . . .
As for me and my household,
we will serve the Lord."

—Joshua 24:15, NIV

CHAPTER ONE

Storm Clouds Gathering

"Through waves and clouds and storms,
He gently clears the way."

—*Give to the Winds Thy Fears*, Paul Gerhardt

The Tornado

The F-4 tornado that touched down at 10:35 p.m. on Sunday, May 4, 2003, in the rural Denmark community in southwestern Madison County, continued on its northeasterly path into downtown Jackson, Tennessee.[1] Leaving a trail of death and destruction, the storm resulted in fourteen fatalities, caused more than 20,000 Jackson Energy Authority customers to lose electricity and water pressure, and inflicted damage or destruction on many buildings.[2] The most notable of those was St. Luke's Episcopal Church, the oldest church in Madison County.

The National Weather Service forecast for that day had called for a combination of sunshine and rain, with a high temperature of 78 degrees.[3] Those of us who attended worship at St. Luke's that morning had not the slightest inkling that within twelve hours our historic church building would be a victim of one of nature's most destructive forces.

Except for the four exterior walls, St. Luke's nave was destroyed. This destruction was not only ominously symbolic of what was going to happen to our fellowship, but also of what was beginning to happen to the Episcopal Church in the United States of America (ECUSA). In the coming months, we would lose something far more precious than our building. We would lose friendships and the fellowship with other believers who worshiped in that building, and it would lead to a situation that we never wanted.

The next day, a warm, sunny Monday, we awoke to the shock of the tornado's widespread devastation. Many of us cautiously navigated the debris-strewn streets to come to the church to begin the long, tedious task of trying to salvage what we could of the things that were damaged: Bibles, hymnals, prayer books, kneelers, and pews. We knew we could build back, but St. Luke's would never be the same.

The Meetings

We were blessed to have a large parish hall that survived the tornado intact. That would serve as our gathering place for worship until the nave could be rebuilt. Late in the summer of 2003, a meeting in that parish hall would begin the process that caused many of us, about one-fourth of St. Luke's parishioners, to leave the church we loved. We embarked on a journey that would lead us to the formation of All Saints Anglican Church.

General Convention—July/August 2003

The event that ultimately led us away from St. Luke's was the General Convention of ECUSA from July 30 to August 8, 2003, in Minneapolis, Minnesota. In a statement dated August 6, 2003, presiding bishop Frank T. Griswold reaffirmed the election of the Rev. Vicky Gene Robinson to be the next bishop in the Diocese of New Hampshire. Griswold described Robinson as being "in a committed relationship with a person of the same sex."[4] In an earlier letter "for all bishops," dated June 12, 2003, Bishop Griswold had stated that some view the election as prophetic and an action of the Holy Spirit, while others view it as disregarding Scripture, tradition, and the larger view of the Anglican Communion, which they see as expressed in a resolution on sexuality of the 1998 Lambeth Conference.[5]

The Lambeth Conference is an assembly of bishops from the Anglican Communion, usually held every ten years, and presided over by the archbishop of Canterbury. That gathering had declared that "this conference cannot advise the legitimizing or blessing of same-sex unions nor ordaining those involved in same-sex unions."[6]

Bishop Griswold further remarked, "While we all accept the authority of Scripture, we interpret various passages in different ways."[7]

At the start of the General Convention of ECUSA in 2003, the Rev. Don Johnson, bishop of West Tennessee, was one of forty-two bishops who stood in opposition to Robinson's election; by the close of the Convention, he had reversed his position.[8] This occurred after the House of Bishops voted to approve the consecration of Robinson.

"The straw that broke the camel's back," Charles Richards recalls, "and why so many of us fled St. Luke's, was that they (General Convention) set all canon law aside to make Robinson a bishop."

Richards recalled that Jeff Garrety, at that time a St. Luke's lay delegate to the General Convention, was in a dinner group at the 2003 Convention.

When Robinson's election was being discussed, Garrety suggested to his group that we "ought to pray about this." A woman sitting next to him responded, "You don't believe that, do you? We have a new revelation."[9]

Bishop Johnson's Visit to St. Luke's—August 2003

On August 13, 2003, our new diocesan Bishop Don Johnson, along with members of the West Tennessee Diocesan Delegation to the General Convention, visited St. Luke's to report on the Convention. They also addressed our concerns about the practices that ECUSA had adopted at that General Convention and that were in contrast to biblical teaching and what we knew to be God's Word. At that meeting, several people asked about Robinson's election. The answers seemed, to many of us, to be an attempt to smooth things over and bring us on board with what was really going on.

Bob Hudson recalls standing in opposition to Robinson's election. He had a rock in one hand and a container of Play-Doh in the other. He asked the bishop if the church had now lost its way: Instead of standing on Scripture as the rock of our faith, had the General Convention taken God's Word and molded it to mean what man says it means, like the Play-Doh? Hudson learned later that Jeannie Johnson, Bishop Johnson's wife, jokingly asked the Rev. Colenzo Hubbard, one of the delegates in attendance, if he would have been willing to stand up and "take one for the bishop" if Hudson had thrown that rock. [10]

In his remarks to us, Bishop Johnson said that we shouldn't worry about a thing; it would be just like women's ordination. "Follow me into the desert," he said, "and we will meet God together."

Malcolm Pearson, who recognized the quote, did not find it encouraging. It wasn't a spiritual journey he was willing to take. He stood and responded, "My family and I will not be going there with you!" [11]

Maida Pearson, Malcolm's mother, drove from Memphis to attend this meeting. She stood and asked, "What about the Bible?" [12]

We were admonished by Charles Crump, a member of the Standing Committee and General Convention delegate, who seemed to imply that we didn't need to be concerned about

Robinson's election and that everything would be okay. Hudson commented later that Crump was correct. We DIDN'T need to be concerned and everything DID turn out okay! [13]

"It was a bad meeting. I was disappointed in Bishop Johnson," recalled Fr. Charles Filiatreau (Fr. Chuck), who was then rector of St. Luke's. [14]

After that meeting, Hudson remembers that the Lord began to put a series of things on his heart, specifically that He wanted Hudson to take a stand and declare whose team he was on. Was he on the traditional Scripture side or the any new man-thought-up-thing-goes side? [15]

Charles Richards recalls that Jim Warmbrod, William Richards, and others left the meeting and went to the adjacent library. He remembers leaving, too, and seeing the others who had left the meeting frustrated and in disbelief at what was happening. [16]

A Place to Stand Conference, October 2003

On October 7-9, 2003, a gathering of concerned Episcopalians from across the nation met in Plano, Texas, a suburb of Dallas. This became popularly known as the Plano Conference. This conference, "A Place to Stand: Declaring, Preparing," saw more than 2,200 attendees come together "to affirm their faith and commitment to the traditional teachings of Scripture in the Anglican Communion and to prepare for realignment of an orthodox Anglicanism in the United States." [17]

The conference was attended by more than 40 Episcopal bishops, 800 priests (including Fr. Chuck), 40 deacons, 100 seminary students, and over 1,500 lay people. [18] Those lay delegates from St. Luke's included Jim Bagley, Brad Box, John Chandler, Gretchen Filiatreau, Jeff Garrety, Tom and Linda Hayes, Bob Hudson, Malcolm Pearson, Billy Slack, and Lloyd Tatum. [19]

A conference highlight was the reading of a message sent by Cardinal Joseph Ratzinger, at that time chief assistant to Pope

John Paul II at the Vatican. Cardinal Ratzinger later became Pope Benedict XVI. The message read:

> From Joseph Cardinal Ratzinger, Prefect of the Congregation for the Doctrine of the Faith, The Vatican, on behalf of Pope John Paul II: I hasten to assure you of my heartfelt prayers for all those taking part in this convocation. The significance of your meeting is sensed far beyond Plano, and even in this City from which Saint Augustine of Canterbury was sent to confirm and strengthen the preaching of Christ's Gospel in England. Nor can I fail to recall that barely 120 years later, Saint Boniface brought that same Christian faith from England to my own forebears in Germany.
>
> The lives of these saints show us how in the Church of Christ there is a unity in truth and a communion of grace which transcend the borders of any nation. With this in mind, I pray in particular that God's will may be done by all those who seek that unity in the truth, the gift of Christ himself.
>
> With fraternal regards, I remain sincerely yours in Christ,
> —Joseph Cardinal Ratzinger [20]

Before the three-day conference concluded, the following statement of faith was endorsed:

> **A Place to Stand: A Call to Action**
> In the Name of the Father, and of the Son, and of the Holy Spirit.
>
> As Anglican Christians committed to the Lordship of Jesus Christ, under the authority of

Holy Scripture, and members of God's one, holy, catholic, and apostolic Church:

1. We proclaim our Lord's Great Commandment and His Great Commission to be our life's highest calling.

2. We repudiate the 74th General Convention's confirmation of a non-celibate homosexual to be a bishop of the Church, and its acceptance of same-sex blessings as part of our common life. These actions have broken fellowship with the larger body of Christ and have brought the Episcopal Church under God's judgment.

3. We repent of our part in the sins of the Episcopal Church, and we pray for all those who are being hurt and led astray by these actions.

4. We call the leadership of the Episcopal Church to repent and reverse the unbiblical and schismatic actions of the General Convention.

5. We declare our commitment to the Lord's life-giving teaching about sexuality and marriage embraced by Christians throughout all ages, and as affirmed by the 1998 Lambeth Conference. We celebrate God's unconditional love for all people, and we proclaim God's transforming power for everyone seeking sexual purity and wholeness.

6. We redirect our financial resources to the orthodox mission and ministry, and away from those structures that support the unrighteous actions of the General Convention. We will support our partners in the Anglican Communion.

7. We appeal to the Anglican Communion primates to intervene in the Episcopal Church to:

   a. Discipline those bishops in the Episcopal

Church who, by their actions, have departed from biblical faith and order;

    b. Guide the realignment of Anglicanism in North America;

    c. Encourage orthodox bishops as they extend Episcopal oversight, pastoral care, and apostolic mission across current diocesan boundaries; and

    d. Support isolated and beleaguered congregations and individuals in their life and witness as faithful Anglican Christians.

To the glory of God. Amen. [21]

St. Luke's Vestry Meeting, November 2003

At this point, it was becoming more and more apparent to many of us that we could not continue to accept things as they were. But what else could we do? We loved our church and our church family and had no desire to leave St. Luke's. At the November 2003 Vestry meeting, a resolution was presented in a last-ditch effort to show unity among the membership at St. Luke's. We needed to take a stand if we were to continue as one body. The resolution read: "The Episcopal Church grievously erred in consecrating a non-celibate homosexual as Bishop and has thereby wounded the body of Christ." [22]

The Vestry voted down the resolution. Lloyd Tatum, a member of the Vestry at the time, resigned as a result of that vote. [23]

In his State of the Church address at the Annual Parish Meeting in December 2003, Fr. Chuck recalled that, at its June 2003 meeting, the Vestry had voted—thirteen for, one against, with one abstention—to inform the bishop and the lay and clerical deputies to the General Convention that St. Luke's Vestry was opposed to the election of V. Gene Robinson. [24] In just a few months, the Vestry had almost completely flipped in its decision to support Robinson's ordination.

Walter Townsend recalled to Fr. Chuck that he remembers walking out of the November Vestry meeting "really distraught" because of the Vestry's failure to uphold the resolution. He phoned Jeff Garrety and asked, "What are we going to do?" Garrety's reply was that those of us who could not, in good conscience, remain in the Episcopal Church needed to start meeting for prayer, repentance, and God's guidance. Townsend immediately offered his home as our gathering place. Townsend and his wife, Jane, were amazed at how many people (forty-six) showed up for that first meeting of food and fellowship.[25]

CHAPTER TWO

Sheep without a Shepherd

" . . . They were weary and scattered, like sheep having no shepherd."

—Matthew 9:36, NKJV

At the Townsends' Home

On November 30, 2003, those who had expressed dismay over what had happened in the Episcopal Church were invited to desserts and hors d'oeuvres at the Townsends' home to share Bible study and conversation about what had happened to our church and what we were being led to do. There were varied opinions and questions: What has happened? When are we leaving? We had a time of prayer, and we sang hymns: "Stand Up, Stand Up for Jesus," "Be Not Afraid," and "A Mighty Fortress." [1]

Our meetings served as an outlet for those who had voiced a collective opinion that we would be leaving St. Luke's. It was clear that we did not want to harm Fr. Chuck by involving him. We decided to use discretion and not discuss things outside the group.

As a result, our meetings were neither gripe sessions nor gossip sessions. Rather, they were modeled after a praise and worship service in the late fall of 2003 at All Saints, Memphis, which several of our number had attended. Many St. Luke's parishioners were already drifting away and others felt at a loss about what to do or where to turn. Called the Gatherings, we adopted the theme Singing the Lord's Praise in a Strange Land.[2]

In her notes taken at the time, Kathy Herriman, now Kathy Trawick, recalled that we shared our dismay, disappointment, disagreement, and distress over the actions of ECUSA and the actions of the General Convention 2003. We questioned how we as Christians committed to the Lordship of Christ, under the authority of Scripture, members of God's one, holy, catholic, and apostolic Church might respond. Going our separate ways was not the answer. We were being called to plant an Anglican church. At that first gathering, each person was asked to read a statement of faith, adapted from the American Anglican Council (AAC), which had been endorsed at the Plano Conference in October. We were asked to sign this statement if so moved.[3]

At our gathering on December 14, we completed surveys to indicate the specific gifts we possessed so that we could use our collective gifts to grow a healthy church.

While still attending St. Luke's on Sunday mornings, we met on Sunday evenings for the rest of the year, except for Christmas week, at the Townsend home.[4] Fr. Chuck said he was aware that these meetings were taking place, but he was not kept informed of exactly what was going on.[5] That was by design; we did not want to jeopardize his position as rector of St. Luke's.

Until we officially left St. Luke's in February 2004, we never held a service that could be seen as competing with theirs.[6] Our usual format was Evening Prayer or Compline accompanied by pianist Joanie Forbes, discussion, fellowship, and refreshments. Forbes was the organist/choirmaster at St. Luke's and was one of the founding members of All Saints. An accomplished musician,

Photo courtesy of All Saints Anglican Church

A small group leading the music at a December 2003 meeting in the Townsend home included Linda Hayes, Bob Hudson, Wendy Googe, Becky Googe, Barbara Hudson, Judy Rose, and Malcolm Pearson. Though small in number, the group had all the parts covered with three sopranos, two altos, one tenor, and one bass.

she had worked most recently with Wright State University, Dayton Opera, and St. Paul's Episcopal Church in Dayton, Ohio.[7]

We maintained a list of prayer needs and were functioning as the Body of Christ. We gathered in the Townsends' den, sitting in an assortment of dining room and kitchen chairs or on the step-down from the dining room into the den.

In a video recalling our first fifteen years, Taylor Laird remembered that we had Books of Common Prayer and hymnals.

"It was so comfortable and peaceful to be in Walter's living room with other people. It was unbelievable. We had been meeting and worshiping and singing," Taylor said. She and her husband, David, had visited other churches. "And I said, 'We don't need to find another church. Aren't we a church? What's going on? What are we doing? You are my people!'"[8]

The rest of us agreed that yes, indeed, we were a church!

Taylor shared with me that while she was struggling with all that was happening within the Episcopal Church, she contacted friends at the Episcopal church where she had grown up, asking them, "What is going on? Isn't the Bible the inerrant Word of God?"

They answered, "No, not necessarily." She lost friends over this; it was a "very big deal" to her.[9]

A church board was proposed and four members were appointed: Jane Garrety, Bob Hudson, Lloyd Tatum, and Walter Townsend. They assumed leadership of our gatherings and met weekly to address questions and to plot a path forward. The board took a straw canvas for stewardship to see if we would be financially able to become a church. The pledged amount was $176,000.[10]

The night we named our church, we had been asked to submit names for our new parish. These names were written across a large dry-erase board. Each of us was given five stars and could place them all on one choice or could distribute them among the various choices. Most of the names recalled early saints in the Christian Church, among them St. Patrick's and St. Luke's Anglican Church. Joe Davis remembers that someone—I believe it was John Herriman—said, "Why don't we just name it All Saints?"[11] His suggestion, All Saints Anglican Church, received the most stars.

Our group of about forty people decided to set February 8, 2004, as our last Sunday at St. Luke's. We informed Fr. Chuck of our decision that we were leaving since we could no longer worship in the Episcopal Church. We asked that no special mention be made of our departure; we would just leave quietly. The only things we took with us were things we owned personally, such as prayer books and serving and choir vestments.[12]

At the Old English Inn

Walter and Jane Townsend had been planning to downsize their living space, and when they found their new home, we needed to find another place to meet. That place turned out to be the Old English Inn.

The Old English Inn had once been a hotel and restaurant before being purchased by Englewood Baptist Church for meeting space. Some of us observed that it was fitting that an Anglican church was meeting at an English inn. We met in a room that opened out onto a patio. Space was cramped, and on at least one occasion, we used part of the patio on an unseasonably warm Sunday. Taylor Laird recalls that she and Lynn Tatum met with the children in another room to have a children's church time. [13]

The room had a piano, and for the first time since leaving St. Luke's, we were able to have a choir. The choir would meet a few minutes before our services started to rehearse the anthem. On one of these Sundays, a couple of Englewood members were in the hallway and heard the choir rehearsing "Alleluia Round" in preparation for that day's service.

"That's a really good choir," one remarked. The other replied, "No, that's a great choir!"

Our youngest attendee was Clare Sprinkle, daughter of founding members Don and Harmony Sprinkle. Clare was about two years old. Charles Richards recalls that at one of our meetings, when we were preparing for the "prayers of the people" portion of the service, Clare shouted out, "Prayer time!" [14] Jane Garrety recalls that, a few weeks later, when it was announced that we had purchased the property at 212 McClellan, Clare shouted, "Amen!" [15]

At that time, we were receiving communion on Sundays, even though we didn't have a priest present to bless the elements. That problem was solved when Jeff Garrety arranged to meet a willing priest from Memphis at Exit 42 off Interstate 40, a halfway point between Memphis and Jackson, receiving from him wine and bread that had been consecrated. There was usually enough to last several Sundays, so there was no need to make weekly trips. [16]

We continued worshiping here throughout March, with the

exception of February 15, our first service in our new building. Our second service at All Saints, and the beginning of our permanent worship at 212 McClellan Road, was Palm Sunday, April 4, 2004.

At the Warmbrods' Home

During Lent, while attending services on Sunday mornings at the Old English Inn, we met with Jim and Halina Warmbrod on Wednesday evenings in their home. [17]

There was a big basement, with a piano, so we were still able to have Joanie Forbes lead our music.

The format remained the same as it had been at the Townsends': Evening Prayer or Compline and a time of fellowship and refreshments.

Looking toward the Future

When the decision was finally made to leave and form our own church, some of us wrote letters to the Vestry and/or staff members of St. Luke's, indicating our impending move and withdrawal of membership and affiliation from St. Luke's. Some of us rescinded any financial pledges we had made to St. Luke's; others completed their pledges. Fr. Chuck recalls that people kept coming to him, telling him that they were leaving. [18] Charles Richards remembers delivering his letter in person to Fr. Chuck, and as he walked out of the church and down the sidewalk, he felt, like Christian in *The Pilgrim's Progress,* that a load had been lifted from his shoulders and that he had done the right thing. [19] Linda Hayes recalls that the letter she and her husband, Tom, wrote to the Vestry described their dismay that derogatory comments had been made regarding the fact that Bishop Githiga, our future bishop, was African. [20]

In a letter to Bishop Johnson dated January 15, 2004, Sally Slack expressed dismay at the diocese's lack of effort "to support the traditional values of the great majority of our Parish." She recalled that the previous December, when her husband, Billy, had been elected to the Vestry, they had made a commitment to stay and "try to fight to regain our church as long as there was hope and clear evidence that the Episcopal Church was actively willing to secure a place for traditional families." She closed with this paragraph:

> I write to you now because I realize my silence might have been interpreted as compliance with the events of General Convention. I am not willing to let that silence tear at my soul any longer. . . . You have an awesome job that God has chosen you for. Please honor and bless Him with your actions. Please behold the Cross and Christ from this ordinary Christian family's perspective. He is not to be "recreated" and updated to suit our whims and consciences. We change to suit Him and bless Him. He does not reside in a big, national office wearing fancy vestments and stoles. He is the Sovereign, Mighty Ruler over all things on this earth and He demands to know, "Who do you say that I am?" [21]

In a 2004 interview with David W. Virtue of VirtueOnline, Fr. Chuck said, "Bishop Don Johnson's pastoral letter was the straw that broke the camel's back. An inclusive church has no place for these orthodox people, and now they have gone. When I try to tell him (the bishop), he listens but never says anything. The greatest feeling I have is sadness. The tornado that destroyed us was a piece of cake compared to what General Convention did to our church." [22]

Bob Hudson told Virtue that the moment of truth for many had come in mid-November when the Vestry of St. Luke's voted down the resolution condemning ECUSA for Robinson's consecration. "People could no longer stand by and watch their witness go up in smoke. The choices were limited: go to another denomination, drive 160 miles roundtrip to Memphis to worship at an Anglican church each week, or form our own Anglican church, so that is what we did." [23]

The founding members began the process of establishing their Anglican affiliation; obtaining a worship space; conducting time, talent, and treasure surveys; establishing teams to deploy the gifts and talents of the parishioners within the community; and all those other necessities of being a church, Virtue reported.

"The National Church (ECUSA) has continued its path toward irrelevance by turning its back on the faith, order, practice, and discipline of the catholic faith," Hudson said in the interview. "As a result, there are families and individuals that can no longer 'wait and see'; they are called to action, to step out in faith."

Hudson described the energy and calling of these individuals in the service of the Lord as being phenomenal.

The gifts and the talents include outreach (both local and international), pastoral care, Christian education, Sunday School teachers, Bible study leaders, choir and choirmaster and organist, Vestry service, senior and junior wardens, chalice bearers, lectors, lay readers, acolytes, altar guild, youth advisors, Alpha course team leaders, and intercessory prayer leaders. [24]

Fr. Chuck said that the orthodox priests still active in the diocese "had their heads on the line because they are standing up for the Gospel." He added that the toll in income at St. Luke's after the breakaway group left would be substantial. At that point, the church had not rebuilt since the tornado, and average attendance was about 200, with some 504 on the rolls. "Our budget will be affected. Because of General Convention, we were already down $30,000; now we expect a deficit of $70,000. Overall the budget has gone from $500,000 to $250,000. I expect my salary will be affected. We were looking for an associate priest but now we can't fund it." [25]

Symptoms of the national church malaise were seen more broadly in West Tennessee in the January 16 Pastoral Letter of the

Rt. Rev. Don Johnson and in his invitation to the Rt. Rev. Chilton Knudsen, bishop of Maine and one of the co-consecrators of V. G. Robinson, to be the keynote celebrant and homilist at the 23rd Annual (West Tennessee) Diocesan Convention on February 20. "This was unacceptable," Hudson said.[26]

What prompted that pastoral letter from Bishop Johnson was an article in the Memphis *Commercial Appeal*, dated January 14, 2004, in which he accused dissenters of using "deceitfulness and subversive sabotage justified in the name of serving Christ." He further stated that the article "outlines publicly the American Anglican Council's (AAC) 'confidential' game plan for the destruction of The Episcopal Church U.S.A. by becoming a 'replacement' jurisdiction, even if it means 'disobedience of canon law on a widespread basis' as deemed necessary." He continued that the AAC's "strategy" seems "to advocate whatever means necessary to 'innovatively move around, beyond, or within the canons' to do so." He outlined several steps he would take to see that this didn't happen, including using his office to determine what steps needed to be taken next regarding "our clergy and congregations formally affiliated with the AAC and its agenda."[27]

Several priests associated with the AAC responded to Bishop Johnson's letter. One of those was the Rev. Dr. Ephraim Radner, senior fellow at The Anglican Communion Institute (ACI), who described the bishop's letter as representing "a consistent ignorance about the Anglican Communion and a willful denial about ECUSA's standing, externally and internally, with respect to its canonical legitimacy in the eyes of both that Communion and many of our own members." He stated further that the AAC's "strategy" that Bishop Johnson referred to in his letter had been public for several months because it represented what the primates of the Global South had proposed to do to discipline ECUSA for going against Scripture. The plan called for the larger Anglican Communion to withdraw its recognition of those bishops who had consented to the election of Bishop Robinson, participated in his consecration, or supported same-sex blessings, and to recognize those who had opposed these measures as the legitimate representatives of ECUSA. He accused the bishops of ECUSA of once again "closing their eyes to what the majority of the Anglican Communion is actually saying, doing, and committed to being." [28]

The official AAC response raised questions about Bishop Johnson's "abuse of the office of bishop by dictating the conscience of Episcopalians in his diocese." The AAC urged the bishop to "refrain from punitive action, harassment, or intimidation of the people under his care who uphold historic Anglican faith and order and whose affiliation with AAC provides them with a place to stand." The response went on to state:

> Bishop Johnson emphasizes his desire to preserve the "church as it currently exists." Here are the facts about the Episcopal Church USA (ECUSA). It is a church that is no longer in relationship with the majority of Anglicans worldwide. It is a church that no longer turns to Holy Scripture for its guidance. It is a church that has chosen the ways of man over the ways of God. It is a church that has undermined the institution of marriage. It is a church with which many worldwide Christian denominations have broken relations. It is a church that has lost its heart and soul and its commitment to making disciples and proclaiming the Good News of Jesus Christ. [29]

PART TWO:
Let Goods and Kindred Go

"Let goods and kindred go, this mortal life also.
The body they may kill; God's truth abideth still.
His kingdom is forever."

—"A Mighty Fortress," Martin Luther

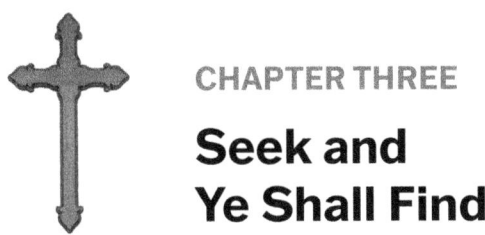

CHAPTER THREE

Seek and Ye Shall Find

"Ask, and it will be given to you; seek, and you will find; knock, and it will be opened to you."

—Matthew 7:7, NKJV

Finding Our Bishop

When it became clear that we would be leaving St. Luke's and starting our own parish, Bob Hudson and Jeff Garrety traveled to Memphis to meet with the Rev. Dr. Samson Gitau, professor of Hebrew and director of Barth House, an Episcopal student house, at the University of Memphis. Their intent was to share with him our undertaking and to ask for his assessment of our actions: Were we being led by the Holy Spirit, or were we traveling on a road to doom? He felt that we seemed to be Holy Spirit-led and agreed to speak with his longtime friend, the Right Reverend Gideon Githiga, bishop of the Anglican Diocese of Thika, and get his perspective and willingness to provide "temporary emergency Episcopal oversight" for our church.[1]

Bishop Githiga was more than qualified to be our bishop. He

had been consecrated as the first bishop of the Thika Diocese in the Anglican Church of Kenya on January 31, 1999. His educational background included a bachelor of divinity degree from St. Paul's Theological College, Limuru, Kenya; a master's degree in sacred theology from General Theological Seminary, New York City; and a doctorate from The Open University in the United Kingdom. His responsibilities included chair of the Provincial Board of Education and Training in the Anglican Church of Kenya; member of the Governing Council of St. Paul's United Theological College in Kenya; and member of the Central Province—Education Board. [2]

Jeff Garrety recalled that the Rev. Dr. Gitau got Bishop Githiga on the phone right then to speak with him. The bishop could not totally understand Garrety's Southern accent, but he understood enough that he was willing to begin a dialogue that would lead to his agreeing to be our bishop. [3] Bishop Githiga, in his first sermon at All Saints, recalled:

"We in Africa benefited from evangelism by the Western missionaries. When Christianity took root, it started spreading like a brush fire. Today, 55 million out of 77 million Anglicans are from the Global South. We now have the opportunity to reciprocate." [4]

In a letter to Bishop Githiga, dated February 10, 2004, in which Garrety requested "immediate Episcopal oversight" for All Saints, he eloquently summed up our position:

> ECUSA has not only separated itself from the body of Christ throughout the world but particularly from Anglicans throughout the world as ECUSA has departed for many years from the authority of Holy Scripture and more recently committed doctrinal error in consecrating a non-celibate homosexual man to the office of Bishop in God's Church, and supported, by laying the groundwork for, the blessing of same-sex unions in contravention of God's Word

> written. While our Bishop, Rt. Rev. Don Johnson, initially voted against the consecration of V. Gene Robinson, his actions and speech since that date have revealed to many believers that West Tennessee is now a hostile diocese.[5]

Hostile, indeed, as Garrety later recalled that first phone conversation with Bishop Githiga. In that conversation, Bishop Githiga asked, "What did Bishop Johnson say when he called you about leaving?"

Garrety replied, "He has not cared or bothered to call." Bishop Githiga agreed that "we had no bishop in a man who would not make a phone call when forty-two Christians said they could not in godly conscience walk with our then-Bishop Johnson. . . . We know what God will give to the double-minded man. Much less, the cry of Elijah in I Kings: 'How long will you stumble between two opinions—if God is God, serve him; if God is Baal, serve him.'"[6]

On the bishop's first visit with us, in June 2004, he privately asked Gretchen Filiatreau, "Did Bishop Johnson ask you why you left the church?" When Filiatreau replied, "No," he said, "Then he doesn't care."[7]

Articles of incorporation were submitted for All Saints Anglican Church, and our charter was officially granted by the state of Tennessee on February 18, 2004. Article Four of that document detailed that our purposes for incorporation are:

> . . . Religious, educational, and charitable in nature and specifically encompass the provision for and the support of the public worship of God; it shall further carry out all proper religious activities in furtherance of the Gospel of Jesus Christ under the authority of Holy Scriptures of the Old and New Testaments as the revealed Word of God in carrying

out our Lord's Great Commandment and His Great Commission in keeping with the historic faith, order, and doctrine of the Anglican Communion as it has accepted the one Holy, Catholic, and Apostolic faith; in keeping with the historic Faith, Order, and Practice as promulgated by the Book of Common Prayer (BCP); the Thirty-Nine Articles of Religion (1801); and the Chicago-Lambeth Quadrilateral, and the Historic Episcopate, and not otherwise.

On February 19, Bishop Githiga granted immediate assistance to All Saints Anglican Church.[8]

All Saints had a sister parish, St. Peter's Anglican Church in Memphis. We were also asked to share evangelism training and youth development with two other Anglican churches in Shelby County.[9]

On June 9, 2004, Bishop Johnson signed a Sentence of Deposition for the Revs. Noland Pipes Jr., Herbert Hand, and Stephen Carpenter, stating that these priests are "deprived of the right to exercise the gifts of spiritual authority conferred in ordination, because of abandonment of the communion of this church by a priest." The Rev. Hand and the Rev. Pipes, priest and associate priest of Faith Anglican Church in Cordova, were now a part of the province of Rwanda. The Rev. Carpenter and his congregation had established St. Peter's Anglican Church in Memphis, which was under the oversight of Bishop Githiga.[10]

Bishop Githiga visited All Saints on June 27, 2004. That Sunday's bulletin described the service as "The Dedication and Consecration of a New Ministry and Holy Eucharist." Appropriately, the processional hymn for that service was "Christ Is Made the Sure Foundation." Much of the service was devoted to the dedication or consecration of the baptismal font, lectern, pulpit, banner, Lord's table, seats, communion vessels, collection vessels, processional cross, church Bible, piano, and the whole

Photo courtesy of All Saints Anglican Church

Bishop Githiga chats with Davis Njoka and Linda Davenport at the Davenport home.

building. (A list of gifts from All Saints members and others is included in the Appendix.) [11]

In his sermon, Bishop Githiga said about his acceptance of our oversight request that he "personally felt that the Lord has been calling me to come over. I have received invitations, but I still feel that it is the Lord authorizing me to come over and give encouragement." He encouraged us to remain firm in our faith in "the Triune God, the Father, the Son, and the Holy Spirit." [12]

In an article he wrote for The American Anglican Council, he said that "moments of uncertainty and confusion have previously occurred in the history of the Christian Church. These moments usually result in renewal and revival. One bishop from here told me that what is happening in the US can only be compared to the Reformation of the sixteenth century." [13]

That evening, we attended a potluck supper to celebrate Bishop Githiga's visit. Gretchen Filiatreau recalls that first visit:

> Our tea expert, Linda Hayes, worked her heart out to make the best pot of tea ever steeped. Over the three days, we noticed not much of it was consumed. There must be some secret to Kenyan tea. When the bishop returned in August 2005, he brought his wife, Mary. I wanted to learn the tea secret. After dinner one evening, I invited Mary into my kitchen and asked her to please make tea for our dessert. Here's her recipe: For two cups of tea, measure 2 cups of boiling water into a saucepan. Add ½ cup milk and bring it to a near boil. Add a teaspoonful of Kenyan tea. I had some. The teaspoon is not a measuring spoon, but one you use for dining. Heat for several seconds. Using a Kenyan strainer—I must have had one—pour tea into a hot teapot. Don't serve with lemon, because it curdles the milk. [14]

During that visit, the Filiatreaus served brunch for forty-four people in their backyard, using "real napkins, real plates, and silver forks." Gretchen Filiatreau remembers that Grace Ann House brought fruit, and Joanie Forbes made cinnamon rolls. Forbes also gave Mary Githiga one of the beautiful, cross-stitched, All Saints framed samplers she had made. [15]

At the church, there was a supper for everyone, and we served goat, a favorite Kenyan dish. Latham's cooked the goat for us. We must have served covered dishes, because Gretchen Filiatreau recalls that she took a spinach salad. [16]

Bishop Johnson had heard of our request for Episcopal oversight from Bishop Githiga. At the Vestry meeting on August 9, 2004, Jeff Garrety reported that Bishop Githiga had sent to Fr.

I Know the Plans I Have for You

Photo courtesy of All Saints Anglican Church

This was the original building on January 8, 2004, when a small group went to check it out as a possible home for All Saints.

Chuck and others a letter in which he related that he had received "a rather lengthy letter from Bishop Johnson strongly advising him to stay out of the Episcopal Diocese of West Tennessee."[17]

In his August 23, 2004, pastoral letter, Bishop Johnson wrote that "the bishop from Thika came to our diocese without my invitation and without my permission to perform Episcopal actions that were beyond his jurisdictional authority." He went on to say that two priests had participated in services with Bishop Githiga, and that he had "inhibited or deposed" four priests for their "abandonment of the communion of this church."[18]

Fr. Chuck was one of those priests.

Finding Our Building

Prior to the events that led to our leaving St. Luke's, Walter Townsend had received a call from a Presbyterian friend who told him that the Memphis Presbytery was preparing to close its church on McClellan Road in Jackson. Townsend shared this information with the Vestry and suggested that they consider this building as a mission church for St. Luke's. The Vestry was not interested. Some time later, when Bob Hudson said that he had a place in mind as a possible church building for us, it so happened that the building was the same one Townsend had suggested to St. Luke's. [19]

That building was Westminster Presbyterian Church on McClellan Road, a church plant from the Memphis Presbytery that had closed because of declining membership. Joanie Forbes remembers getting a call from Jeff Garrety, asking her to join him and others to see a church building they were considering for us. He gave her directions and asked if she would call Townsend. Townsend's arthritis was acting up, so Forbes offered to take him to the church. She remembers walking into the building with members of the negotiating team, prior to our purchase of the property, to assess whether the building would be suitable for our needs.

"It had been raining a lot, and there must have been roof leaks, as the carpet was full of puddles, and the floor was a mess. Someone said the carpet would be changed. That's a good start, I thought," Forbes said. "Then I saw a grand piano on the stage. They told me it would stay, and I explained why it would have to be moved. There was a small room where we would keep our vestments and music cabinets. We would have a choir. Things were looking up and getting better!" [20]

We began negotiations with the Memphis Presbytery in early 2004. The original asking price for the building, its contents, and the ten acres on which it sat was $1,080,000. After a series of offers and counteroffers, we were finally able to purchase the building on April 28, 2004, after Fr. Chuck became our rector, for the price of $667,500. [21]

The presbytery agreed to allow us to hold a worship service at the church on February 15, 2004, so we could determine whether the facility would work for us. Prior to that service, we scheduled a cleaning day. Forbes recalls that she and I cleaned the ladies' room.[22] There were eighty-five people in attendance that first Sunday in what was to become our new church home. At that service, we blessed communion vessels and linens donated by some of our members, along with a chalice and paten, presented by the Rev. Noland Pipes and his wife, Mary. That first service was followed by a fellowship luncheon at the Warmbrods' home.[23]

Our membership ranged in age from toddler to over eighty. Some of us were cradle Episcopalians, and some grew up in other denominations—Baptist, Catholic, Methodist, and Presbyterian. Some were new to the faith. Some were fairly new to the Jackson area, and some had lived in the area all their lives. There were singles, couples with children, couples with grown children, couples with no children, and grandparents.[24]

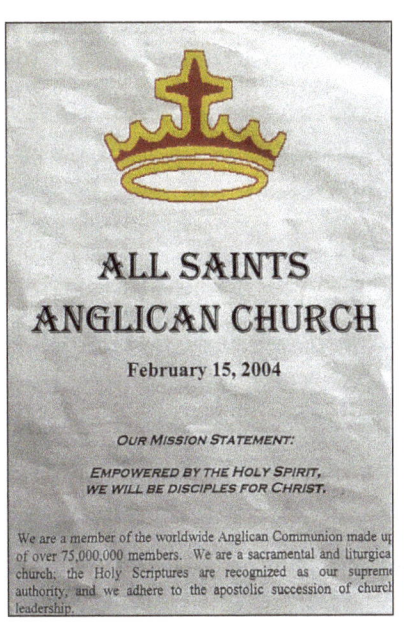

Photo courtesy of Judy Rose
Our first Sunday service bulletin was on February 15, 2004.

The bulletin for that service was only four pages long. The front page proudly proclaimed our mission statement: "Empowered by the Holy Spirit, we will be disciples for Christ." The back page welcomed attendees to "the First Eucharist of All Saints Anglican Church." Hymns that day included "A Mighty Fortress," which had become our unofficial theme song, especially this portion of verse four: "Let goods and kindred go; this mortal life also; the body they may kill; God's truth abideth still." We had a choir, and Bob and Barbara

Hudson donated chime bars for canting. We sang an anthem, "I Am the Resurrection."

The Rev. Noland Pipes, from Memphis, was the preacher and celebrant that day. Serving were Joanie Forbes, choirmaster; Linda Hayes, cantor; Jim Bagley, chalice bearer; Barbara Hudson and Lloyd Tatum, lectors; Jim and Halina Warmbrod, ushers; John and Kathy Herriman, greeters; and Andrew Wagner, acolyte. Bob and Shirley Phillips gave the altar flowers in thanksgiving for our parish. We already had a prayer chain, and parishioners were directed to report critical prayer needs to Linda Hayes. [25]

We had not yet officially bought the property, so we continued worshiping at Old English Inn until Palm Sunday, April 4, when we could finally put our name on the sign and move in. Since we had no priest yet, we had no sermons for these services, but Garrety was able to get sermons from a couple of priests we trusted, and those sermons were read at our Old English Inn services.

Finding Our Priest

The journey that eventually brought Fr. Chuck to All Saints began when he was a student at the University of Arkansas and began to feel that the Lord was calling him to ministry in the Episcopal Church. He accepted that call and graduated from Virginia Theological Seminary with a master of divinity degree in 1968. He was ordained to the deaconate on June 18, 1968, and to the priesthood on March 27, 1969. He has served as vicar at Calvary Episcopal Church in Osceola, Arkansas; as rector and headmaster of Holy Cross Episcopal Church and Day School in West Memphis, Arkansas; and as rector of St. Luke's Episcopal Church in Jackson. [26]

In January 2004, Fr. Chuck had been hospitalized for stress-related issues, and he began contemplating retirement from St. Luke's and from the priesthood in ECUSA.

In his letter to the people of St. Luke's dated May 3, 2004, he announced his impending retirement, effective

May 31, 2004. He wrote that the decisions and directions of the General Convention in August 2003 forced him to wrestle with "what are the sources of authority in my life—Holy Scripture, tradition, and reason, or experience, man, and culture. . . . It was very clear through prayer and spiritual direction that the mental, spiritual, and emotional stress of being in an adversarial relationship with ECUSA, my bishop, and many members of the parish is not what God is calling me to do. . . . Therefore, I have chosen early retirement."[27]

In a letter to the editor of the *Jackson Sun*, published on May 11, 2004, Jackson resident Preston G. Atkinson commented on Fr. Chuck's decision:

> As I picked up the Wednesday newspaper, I had no idea that I would experience heroism in a man who stands against what has become the norm, not only in culture, but eventually the Christian Church. This is the kind of news worthy of history and bedtime stories for children so that they might have examples of integrity. Where are the men and women who stand for absolute truth, its authority and a willingness to become a servant of scorn against the cultural trends?
>
> I honor Fr. Chuck Filiatreau for his stand for biblical integrity against the growing tidal wave of tolerance of the wrong kind. It is one thing to love and speak the truth about Scripture, but it is an entirely different thing to say "whatever," an "anything goes" type of tolerance.
>
> "Well, times have changed," some might say. Well, Scripture has not and is not relative to our times and culture. Either all Scripture is authoritative for the church or it is not. If it is not,

one does not have a church but rather a club that is tossed about like driftwood.

Thank you, Fr. Chuck, for your example and service to the universal church. I will tell my children of the stand you have taken. [28]

When his retirement was announced, at least three entities in addition to All Saints approached Fr. Chuck about employment with them. One offer was as a missionary to Venezuela. Suzy McCall, our missionary in Honduras, asked him about coming to the LAMB Institute there. An organization in Jackson also asked him to join its staff. [29]

In the meantime, a Priest Search Process Committee had been formed at All Saints, and we began actively looking for a priest. Those on the committee were Jane Garrety, David Laird, Jane Townsend, Debbi Wagner, and Jim Warmbrod. [30]

At a meeting on March 17, 2004, the search committee made plans to distribute copies of "Who are we?" and "Who is our rector?" to the congregation on the next Sunday and request the members take them home, read them, and make comments and suggestions by the following Sunday. Board members would take that feedback into consideration as they finalized the documents that would result in our choice for rector. They would also include the names of potential candidates anyone would like to have considered for the position. [31]

It had been on the minds of many of us since our leaving St. Luke's that Fr. Chuck was the one we wanted for our priest. Joe Davis recalls that he prayed for this to happen. [32] Many of us privately prayed for the same thing, especially after learning that he had retired from St. Luke's and from the priesthood in ECUSA. At some point, we were asked to submit names of priests we might approach about accepting a call to be our first rector. Fr. Chuck was overwhelmingly the top choice. Fr. Chuck, however, was

Photo courtesy of All Saints Anglican Church

Fr. Chuck, shown above with Gretchen Filiatreau, joined All Saints as rector after he retired from St. Luke's Episcopal Church.

not leaving St. Luke's without a clear word from the Holy Spirit. Walter Townsend remembers hearing that Gretchen Filiatreau would frequently ask Fr. Chuck, "Has the Holy Spirit spoken to you yet?"[33] Apparently, the Holy Spirit had already spoken to her!

When Jim Warmbrod approached him about becoming our rector, Fr. Chuck told him that he would need some time to think about this. After all, he had just retired and needed time off from all the events that had recently occurred at St. Luke's and within ECUSA. He was still recovering from his hospitalization in January. In addition, the search committee wanted a strong youth program, and he wasn't sure he could provide that. He told Warmbrod and the others who had approached him with job offers that he would wait until after the Honduras mission event in May to make his decision.[34]

The time off Fr. Chuck wanted never materialized. By that time, we had found our bishop and our need for a priest was pressing, especially since Bishop Githiga was planning to visit us in June. Fr. Chuck accepted the call, knowing that it was God's will.

Joanie Forbes remembers the phone call she received from Fr. Chuck, telling her that he was going to be our first rector.

"He was going to be my boss again, and Gretchen would be singing alto in the choir again! I knew then that All Saints would become a bit of Heaven here on Earth. With Fr. Filiatreau here, and all the parishioners working along, we would surely grow in the right direction. This was the best news ever." [35]

Fr. Chuck's and Gretchen's first Sunday with us was glorious, with many smiles and hugs being exchanged as we were reunited after what seemed like a very long time, when in reality, it had been only a few months. A reception followed the worship service. Their thank-you note to the parish sums up how they felt:

> With the help and guidance of the Holy Spirit and a great deal of hard work, you have brought together a new body of Christ so obviously eager to do His work in the world. Your initial board did exceptional work and deserves considerable commendation.
>
> We are delighted and grateful to be here and we look forward to the work we will accomplish together through the power of the Holy Spirit for His glory.
>
> Surely the presence of the Lord is in this place. [36]

CHAPTER FOUR

The Lord Works in Mysterious Ways

"And we know that all things work together
for good to those who love God,
to those who are called according to His purpose."
—Romans 8:28, NKJV

The Underground Church

Gretchen Filiatreau wrote this chapter, except for this paragraph. When I asked her to write down some of her memories of those early days, I didn't anticipate how generous she would be with her time and effort in fulfilling the task. This portion of what she wrote was just wonderful and is such an in-depth look at what was happening from her perspective that I didn't want to lose cohesiveness by breaking her words apart and including her writing in other places in the book.

"This was uncharted territory," Gretchen Filiatreau recalled. "The Episcopal Church was the first denomination to splinter over its plans to consecrate a practicing gay man as a bishop and its rejection of Scripture in Leviticus 18:22."

August 2000

Chuck and I attended the Episcopal Church national General Convention in Denver. Bishops and laymen were dividing between conservative biblical views and liberal attitudes outside of the Gospel. Our bishop, Jim Coleman, voted on the biblical side. The diocesan lay delegates were divided.

The daily opening prayer service was so off base and so lacking in meaningful spirituality (like Jesus Christ) that we attended a small prayer service conducted by Bishop Bob Duncan, who later spearheaded the move to the Anglican Church and became archbishop of the Anglican Church in North America (ACNA).

In our free time, we attended meetings with a Trinity Seminary group to discuss the alarming trends and what to do. We did not discuss this upon returning to St. Luke's because we figured they wouldn't believe us. We were right.

August 2003

Jeff Garrety attended the next national meeting for the final vote on the consecration. His statement: "I wouldn't have believed it if I hadn't seen it for myself." We know now that God sent him to the meeting.

Our new diocesan bishop, Don Johnson, voted against the consecration. I telephoned his wife, Jeanie, to applaud his action and encourage her to stand by him and support him in his unpopular decision. The next news was that the bishop had reversed himself and voted "yes." Some believed that he gave in to serious diocesan financial threats from large Memphis churches. People's comments: "Oh, this is a national church thing. It can't happen here."

Bishop Johnson "toured" churches in his diocese to gain support, bringing along the chancellor and several clergymen. At St. Luke's, there was an unsatisfactory question-and-answer session. Maida Pearson asked, "What about the Bible?"

When Jane Townsend asked what we should do, Fr. Reynolds

Cheney (Holy Communion) replied, "I'm not going to tell you how to dismantle the Episcopal Church!"

Bishop Johnson closed the meeting with a brief talk inviting us all to join him in wandering through the wilderness without knowing where our journey might lead. I was reminded of the Israelites who failed to believe God would overcome their enemies in the Promised Land. When they disobeyed the Lord, He sentenced them to a forty-year hike in the wilderness that ended in death for an entire generation.

As Chuck preached against the action of the national church, opposition increased. Some believed the best way to combat the problem was to remain and fight from within. A St. Luke's member wrote a letter to the *Jackson Sun*, calling the Bible group "Pharisees." It was one of many times that I wanted to respond out loud. Chuck always said, "No, you can't do that." I am so grateful that he stopped me every time.

Not knowing the future, we decided to go ahead with our plan to buy our church-owned home. The sale had to be approved by the Diocesan Executive Committee. In Chuck's experience, this was a simple rubber stamp. He wasn't even going to the meeting. However, the Holy Spirit intervened, and he decided to go. Meeting with the committee was a St. Luke's member whom we considered to be a good friend. He said, "Don't sell him this house. He's just going to go out and start another church in competition with St. Luke's." Chuck still had no intention of going anywhere. Through the Holy Spirit, Chuck prevailed, and the sale was approved.

As you've read elsewhere, the "underground church" set a February 2004 date for its last Sunday. With great kindness, each one visited Chuck to say they weren't leaving because of him.

Everyone who remained at St. Luke's was not hostile, but there were enough snubs and glares to make one uncomfortable. As time went on, the atmosphere grew worse until I felt the hatred was palpable.

One of the goals of this group (the underground church) was to prevent Chuck from being deposed. Thus, no one who left contacted him or told him about their plans or meetings. He could honestly say he didn't know anything about it. For example, one Sunday morning, a parishioner asked him, "Are you going to the meeting tonight?" Puzzled, Chuck answered, "What meeting?"

The underground group began to send us "Thinking of You" cards as a way to encourage us. There was no news enclosed, but the cards were greatly appreciated.

When Chuck was at work, Jeff Garrety called to learn if he had decided what to do about leaving the church or staying. He also explained the underground church's efforts to avoid Chuck's being deposed. Obviously, I could not repeat anything I learned nor mention Garrety's calls. I never did, because I, too, did not want him to be deposed.

As an aside, I'll say here that there were people inside St. Luke's and people outside the church who were convinced that Chuck planned the whole departure and All Saints itself. Ironically, much of the news Chuck learned came from Bishop Johnson himself.

Garrety urged me to encourage Chuck to make up his mind. The new church would need a priest. If Chuck was unavailable, they'd find someone else. Chuck had received offers to work at the Episcopal Cathedral in Caracas, Venezuela, to work with Suzy McCall in Honduras, and to join the staff of an evangelical group in Jackson, for example. I had waited upon the Lord for long periods before. But this time I was impatient and had to ask forgiveness. I knew what I wanted, but I didn't know what God wanted. I wouldn't try to influence Chuck, because God had called him to the ministry. Chuck had to wait upon the Lord so that we would remain in God's will.

Every week or so, I asked, "Have you heard from God yet?"

"No," Chuck answered.

During this time of upheaval and lots of tossing and turning at night, I gave myself a treat. I visited the underground church service once in the Warmbrods' basement. It was a true joy.[1] (Marty Courcelle recalls that Gretchen Filiatreau told her, "He [Fr. Chuck] finally released me!")[2]

At a St. Luke's Vestry meeting, one man announced, "I think it's time for Chuck to leave." Perhaps that was the turning point.

At last, Chuck told me he had decided to take early retirement. The diocese called several times to remind him that he could not take his discretionary fund with him, which he knew, of course. He gave it to the outreach committee.

Shortly thereafter, around April 28, 2004, Joanie Forbes called to say the new church had been purchased, the Presbyterian Church building with the green roof at 212 McClellan Road. She invited me to come and see it. "It's okay. Chuck knows. It looks like a church in New England. You'll love it!" She was right. I did love it straight away. It was a lovely little white building with a fetching green roof. Inside, it was white, bright, and light with gleaming brass chandeliers. There were no shutters then, so the sun came shining through. All it needed was a communion rail. It was simple. It was beautiful. It was home.

The inescapable conclusion is that All Saints was founded by the Holy Spirit using the work of laymen and without a benefit of clergy, except indirectly.

Jeff Garrety and the Steering Committee (Jane Garrety, Bob Hudson, Lloyd Tatum, and Walter Townsend) knew exactly what to do. Garrety called Bishop Gideon Githiga in Kenya to ask for oversight. The group secured a reduction in the price of the property, a fully furnished church. They knew to arrange for incorporation, write a constitution, form a Vestry, choose a new name, arrange for services and servers, set up an altar, secure approved sermons to be read, and secure blessed sacrament. The last was full of intrigue and sounded like contraband. A Memphian, bringing the elements, would meet someone from Jackson halfway.

Over the next couple of years, Chuck and I attended numerous Anglican organizational and inspirational meetings around the country. We listened to many stories of other churches, still trying to find a permanent meeting place, still packing and unpacking an altar every Sunday and storing it all week, some still in conflict with their former church. All had the benefit of clergy.

Why was All Saints so fortunate and so blessed? The most we can say is that God works in mysterious ways, and we'll never know why. "Why" is the Lord's business. We must remember it was the Holy Spirit who established All Saints. He deserves all the glory. We are committed to follow His leading and remain always in His will, doing what He wants and not what we want. Our love and gratitude should be overflowing for such a blessing.

In August 2004, Bishop Johnson did depose Chuck and prohibited him from performing any priestly services on Episcopal Church property. I cannot speak to what that action cost Chuck. I do know he has risen above it and bears no ill will toward anyone.

I believe this schism made possible for all the founders the fulfillment of Matthew 5:11—"Blessed are you when men shall revile you, and persecute you, and say all manner of evil against you falsely for my sake." Underline "falsely" and "for Jesus's sake." It is the one time in my life when I felt like I had really done something for Jesus. One of the most precious memories of our early church was an inner assurance during services. ". . . they were all with one accord in one place." (Acts 2:1)

The schism itself brings to mind Isaiah 5:20: "Woe unto them that call evil good, and good evil; that put darkness for light, and light for darkness; that put bitter for sweet, and sweet for bitter!" [3]

CHAPTER FIVE

Our Kenyan Connection

"God, I thank you for Bishop Githiga and his supportive friend, Archbishop Nzimbi, for their care and oversight of us. Give us strength to show our love for Christ, our hearts for the Christians in Kenya who have reached out to us in Christian love and care."
—Jeff Garrety, journal entry, April 6, 2005

Until the formation of the International Diocese and the Province of the Anglican Church in North America (ACNA) in 2009, we remained under the oversight of the Anglican Diocese of Thika, Province of Kenya, and the Right Reverend Bishop Dr. Gideon Githiga.

Visits from Kenya to All Saints

During those years, All Saints clergy and laity made several trips to Kenya, and Bishop Githiga visited us several times as well. His first visit was in June 2004, followed by two more: one in January 2007 and the other in September 2007.[1] On the January 2007 visit, Githiga brought with him Kenyan Archbishop Benjamin Nzimbi.

Photo courtesy of Jeff Garrety

Lynn Tatum, second from left, Linda Hayes, second from right, and Jeff Garrety, far right, enjoy the company of two Kenyan friends in 2007.

On January 8, 2007, Bishop Githiga and Archbishop Nzimbi arrived in Jackson on their first of several stops in the United States before heading back home. The *Jackson Sun* had been contacted about the archbishop's impending visit and wrote a very positive article, inviting everyone to come and hear the archbishop preach.

While in Jackson, Bishop Githiga and Archbishop Nzimbi were guests at a special dinner on Saturday evening, January 13, in the home of Dr. Rich and Debbi Wagner, to which All Saints parishioners were invited to give us all a chance to meet the archbishop. On Sunday morning the archbishop confirmed new members to our church family. [2]

Jordan Tang recalls that on one of Bishop Githiga's visits to Jackson (probably the one in September 2007), he attended the Starlight Symphony, performed by the Jackson Symphony, which was at that time conducted by Dr. Tang. Becky Googe and Sarah Beth Hanson, members of the symphony and of All Saints, asked him to announce Bishop Githiga's presence, which he did. [3]

I Know the Plans I Have for You

Photo courtesy of All Saints Anglican Church

All Saints members visit Kenya, April 7, 2005. Pictured, left to right, are Rich Wagner, Bob Hudson, Fr. Chuck, Archbishop Benjamin Nzimbi, Bishop Gideon Githiga, Jeff Garrety, and Mary Githiga.

"It was always a pleasure to see him [Bishop Githiga]," Gretchen Filiatreau commented. "We could never thank him enough for taking us in when we needed a home."[4]

We were also blessed by a visit from the bishop's brother, John Githiga, who came from Texas for a three-day stay in August 2004. And in October 2008, we enjoyed a visit from our new African friends, Joshua and Alice Nguria.

"Of course we served Kenyan tea. I was so proud we could do it," Filiatreau said.[5]

Visits from All Saints to Kenya

In keeping with the Anglican tradition, 10 percent of our yearly budget went to our diocese, which was Thika, Kenya, and on at least one occasion, our Easter offering was donated to the diocese.

The $2,075 Easter offering of 2005 was one of the largest presented that year at Harambee—a Kenyan tradition of fundraising or development activities. Also, two members of the All Saints delegation that year made a $10,000 donation. In 2007, Linda Hayes, who was a delegate, was selected to present our gift, which "she did with some beautiful words of gratitude to Bishop Githiga."[6]

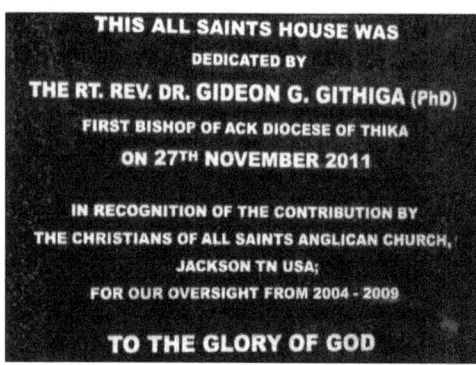

Photo courtesy of All Saints Anglican Church
The All Saints House sign displayed in Thika, Kenya, 2013.

Bishop Githiga had a reputation for being a good manager, and he saved these funds and added more to them until there was enough money to construct a sixteen-unit apartment building for the people of Thika. This building was named All Saints House, and representatives from All Saints were there the day it was dedicated. In 2013, members of our All Saints delegation were honored to see All Saints House.[7]

On his 2007 trip to Kenya, Fr. Chuck became very ill with what was believed to be a stomach virus. Linda Hayes and Lynn Tatum, who accompanied him and other delegates that year, helped nurse him back to health. Back home, we all prayed for him and were so relieved when he returned home.

CHAPTER SIX

The Move

"Get out of your country . . .
to a land that I will show you."
—Genesis 12:1, NKJV

Adjusting to Our New Home

Once we had made our final offer and the Memphis Presbytery had accepted it, we began the process of moving into our new space. The building contents included almost everything we needed to start worshiping there. A piano, altar table, baptismal font, chairs, and some altar furnishings were there as well as office, nursery, and kitchen furniture and supplies. Individuals were asked to donate hymnals and prayer books, which we gladly did.

Anne Rushing remembers the Sunday when we dedicated our property and all the items to be used for our worship. We walked around the nave, stopping periodically to pray for each thing.[1]

There were no altar hangings, so the church bought these piece by piece as the church seasons and colors changed. We also purchased vestments for clergy, acolytes, lay eucharistic ministers

(LEMs), and chalice bearers, gradually and over time. The large wooden cross that hung behind our altar—and hangs in the new nave as well—was given in honor of Walter and Jane Townsend. Rich and Debbi Wagner donated the processional cross in memory of their son, Matthew, who had died at the age of six months while we were still at St. Luke's. Bob and Barbara Hudson donated the ambry and ambry candle. People in the parish donated altar utensils in thanksgiving or in memory of loved ones. There were no choir vestments either, so Joanie Forbes ordered them. Several of us had brought from St. Luke's the wooden crosses that a fellow choir member had made years before to wear with our vestments.

Caroline Crumpton, a cousin of William and Charles Richards, donated the antique gold cross on the table at the back of the nave in memory of Louise Richards and Adrienne Jones. The cross came from a church in Minnesota.[2]

Joanie Forbes and Debbi Wagner are responsible for the All Saints banner, which is still displayed in the chancel. Forbes remembers:

> One day it came to me: we needed a banner. So I went home and did lots of homework. What it should say, colors, etc. In a conversation with Debbi Wagner, I mentioned that we needed a banner. I have all the symbols for the design and know the colors it needs to be, but where would I find the 'churchy' fabric it needs? So off we went to Memphis. I purchased the fabric and was happy with it, but then I remembered that it needed to be put together. Debbi said she could do it. With three children in school, a husband, and a huge house to care for, Debbi had too much to handle, so asking her wasn't fair. I should find someone else. Debbi had already been a huge help finding the fabric

I Know the Plans I Have for You 51

Photo courtesy of All Saints Anglican Church
This was the chancel area of the original building, January 8, 2004.

shop. So every person I talked to recommended Dixie Berryman. She did this for other churches and would be glad to help us. Then I realized we needed hardware for the banner, something that it would hang on and that the acolytes could use to carry it into services. Bob Hudson learned of this need and made it himself. When I offered to pay him for it, he said it was free.[3]

In the beginning, and at least through 2013, we had an American flag and a Christian flag that were prominently displayed on either side of the altar area. Both flags were donated by Bob and Shirley Phillips.[4]

Jeff and Jane Garrety donated the sign in our parking lot that welcomes people to All Saints with the invitation from Matthew 11:28, "Come to me, all who labor and are heavy-laden, and I will give you rest." On the other side, which we see upon leaving the parking lot, we are reminded that we are "now entering the mission field."

Although not arriving until years later, the beautiful Steinway baby grand piano that we enjoy hearing each Sunday was a gift from Dr. Harris Lake Smith, bequeathed to us in his will in 2016. Harris loved music and was quite an accomplished pianist, so this gift of one of his most treasured possessions says volumes about how much he loved his church and church family.

In 2012, a columbarium was installed behind the altar table beneath the cross donated in honor of the Townsends. This columbarium was relocated to the new nave.

Another early addition was that of a votive candle stand where parishioners can light a candle and offer prayer requests. This was made by Kenny Hanson and donated to All Saints by Kenny and Sarah Beth in memory of her mother. This also was moved to the new nave. A more complete list of gifts, some with added details, can be found in the Appendix.

We could not afford to pay a sexton (custodian) in the beginning, so we had a church cleanup day when we all showed up to dust, vacuum, mop, and clean the kitchen and bathrooms. We would periodically have work days until we were able to hire someone. There was a cleanup schedule that assigned monthly cleanup duties to our four small groups on a rotating basis. This schedule was in place at least through October 2004. The minutes from the December 6, 2004, Vestry meeting reported that Sarah Beth Hanson cleaned our church weekly as a volunteer. [5]

We couldn't afford a lawn service either, so when the weather got warmer, the workdays included pruning, trimming, raking, and mowing the church grounds as well as cleaning the church. In his report to the Annual Parish Meeting in December 2004, Bill Boggs, coordinator of buildings and grounds, thanked Duane Rushing, Frank Ewing, Bronson Doyle, Bob Hudson, and Kenny Hanson for "taking care of our ten plus acres of land." [6]

In 2005, a garden guild was formed, with Walter Townsend

and David Nailling as co-chairs. Other members of the All Saints Garden Guild were Linda Davenport, Julia Nailling, Carlin Diffee, Rita Davis, Ruth Oliver, Melinda Pearson, Joanna Priester, Billy Slack, Halina Warmbrod, Kathy Herriman, Bronson Doyle, Kenny Hanson, and Debbi Wagner.[7]

Gretchen remembers that in the beginning there was no fence separating All Saints' property and University School of Jackson's property. After Easter one year, Lynn Tatum brought some baby ducks to USJ's pond for their new home. She also brought feed. Since Lynn couldn't always be there to feed the ducks, Fr. Chuck either fed the ducks himself or found someone else to feed them when he couldn't. As the ducks grew older, we would sometimes see them waddle from the pond, cross the parking lot, and mill about the church door, waiting for someone to feed them. "It was an endearing sight as long as it lasted."[8]

Settling into our new building meant the beginning of new habits and practices. One habit that some of us developed was greeting one another by saying, "God is good," to which the other would respond, "All the time."

Another practice involved the use of our name tags. Bob Hudson made a small wooden rack that held a permanent name tag for each parishioner. This rack hung on the wall just inside the main entrance to the building. On Sunday mornings, we would reach for our name tags as we entered the church. We wore these to identify ourselves to visitors.

Andy Hudson was in charge of the name tag board and made sure we all got our name tags upon entering the building. Occasionally, someone would make it past Andy without getting his name tag, and Andy would take it to that person in the nave. Andy also made sure we returned our name tags to the board before leaving the building.

One tradition we brought from St. Luke's was the folding of palm crosses. On the Saturday before Palm Sunday, everyone was invited to come to the church to help make small crosses from palm branches to be distributed the next day.

Another notable tradition we brought with us from St. Luke's was the flowering of the cross at Easter. This had been started by eight to ten mothers who had lost children. The two mothers who saw that the tradition continued at All Saints were Debbi Wagner and Courtney Davison. Debbi began with a cross of gnarled, real tree limbs. This was deemed to be too difficult for the children to attach the flowers, however, so Jake Stewart made the cross we use today.

Since the flowering is a memorial to lost children, it is not just a "nice thing" to do at Easter. It is important to remember parts of our history such as this, so that we do not lose the deeper meaning of the tradition.[9]

I remember well our first Christmas Eve in our "new" church building. It was cold and there was ice and snow on the ground, making the roads treacherous. We had looked forward to this special service for many weeks—the choir especially, because we had rehearsed for months the music we would be singing for our Festal Choral Eucharist that night. Fr. Chuck and his team of "florists" had spent hours beautifully decorating the church for Christmas Eve and Christmas Day.

I lived in Medina at the time, and there was no way I would venture out on those slick roads by myself. The Pearson family came to my rescue. They lived in Medina, too, and Malcolm was a fellow choir member, so I was able to ride with them to church that night. Our crowd was slim, but we celebrated Christ's birth with much joy and thanksgiving for all the ways God had blessed us that year.

Making Changes

The most notable immediate change was in the chancel area. When we began worshiping at All Saints, the piano was on the left side of this area. The choir was on the other side, facing the piano.

Photo courtesy of All Saints Anglican Church

Parishioners with palm branches processed around the church on Palm Sunday, March 30, 2015.

The altar table was in the center but a little closer to the congregation. There was no altar rail, no ambry, or no hymn board. When Fr. Chuck became our rector, two of the first things he did were to change the location of the piano to a place near the back of the nave, behind the congregation, and to have an altar rail built.

In the beginning, the current rector's office was where the

Vestry met. There was no table, just a seven-foot-long sofa and some chairs. The smaller office adjacent to the main church office was the rector's office. After our "flood" in 2010, the rector's office was moved to its current location. The Vestry met in the large room across from the nursery. That room had originally been used for the youth. The two rooms where children's church meets were originally one room. In 2006, a partition was installed to make it into two rooms. The All Saints Immigration Services (ASIS) office used to be the area used for toddlers.

PART THREE:
The Lord Will Guide Your Feet

"He will not allow your foot to be moved;
He who keeps you will not slumber."
—Psalm 121:3, NKJV

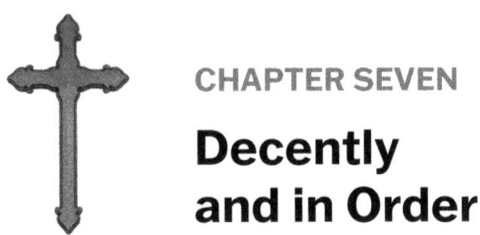

CHAPTER SEVEN

Decently and in Order

"Let all things be done decently and in order."
—I Corinthians 14:40, NKJV

Our Board

Before Fr. Chuck became our rector, our leadership consisted of a board of directors who led us into the unfamiliar territory of forming a new church. Serving on that board were Jane Garrety, Bob Hudson, Lloyd Tatum, and Walter Townsend. Joanie Forbes remembers that the work they did was unbelievable and done so well. It seemed they could solve any problem that popped up. I never heard a grumble or complaint from them. Soon All Saints was a parish and a family.[1]

After Fr. Chuck became our rector, a Vestry was commissioned on June 20, 2004.[2]

Our First Vestry

A look back at the Vestry meeting minutes from those early days at All Saints reveals that we took very seriously Paul's directive in I Corinthians 14:40 to "Let all things be done decently and in order." We prayed about and discussed everything and made decisions based upon the guidance of the Holy Spirit. We were intent upon "keeping the main thing the main thing." Our first meeting was on July 12, 2004,[3] and our first Vestry retreat was held at the church on Saturday, July 17, 2004.[4]

As a new Vestry, most of us were in uncharted waters since we had never before been the "first" Vestry in a new parish. (See the Appendix for the names of the first Vestry members.)

Thankfully, Fr. Chuck and other leaders wanted to be sure that we were proceeding in the right direction and making Spirit-led decisions. We underwent spiritual gifts and work style patterns inventories to see where each Vestry member's strengths lay so that we could all work together as a cohesive unit to help carry out the mission of our church. Each member of the Vestry had a specific duty to perform, based upon his/her spiritual gifts.

> "Empowered by the Holy Spirit, we will be disciples for Christ."
>
> All Saints mission statement

It became clear to us that God had provided our Vestry with a variety of gifts—in fact, every spiritual gift we needed to fulfill our purpose. And not only that, members of the church as a whole brought something that could be used for the body. Not surprisingly, God knew what we needed before we did. As Isaiah 65:24 states, "Before they call, I will answer, while they are yet speaking, I will hear."

That first Vestry was composed of eight parishioners; four would serve one year and four would serve two years. That meant that half of the Vestry would rotate off one year and the other half would rotate off the second year. That way, there would always be a balance between "new" Vestry and "old" Vestry members (except for the first Vestry).

Who We Are

As a Vestry, we spent time developing and adopting a mission statement that clearly said what we were all about, and everything we did reflected that: "Empowered by the Holy Spirit, we will be disciples for Christ." We wanted everything we did to reflect Christ.

In his capacity as rector's warden, Jeff Garrety said at our December 6, 2004, Vestry meeting that he felt the excitement at All Saints that comes from being a healthy and well-balanced church. "We are teaching the Word, our outreach is active, and everyone in leadership is doing well. God's presence is felt here. When we worship in spirit and in truth, as we do, people will feel that way when they visit."[5]

In September 2004, the Vestry identified characteristics of healthy, well-balanced New Testament churches and endorsed the following membership expectations:

1. Members of All Saints are baptized.
2. Members have a relationship with Jesus as their personal Savior.
3. Members regularly attend church.
4. Members are actively involved in parish ministry.
5. Members are committed to moving toward the biblical minimum of a 10 percent tithe.
6. Members are committed to unity in the church and to refrain from gossip.
7. Members will actively participate in small sharing groups.
8. Members are committed to the Great Commission.
9. Members strive to lead a godly life.
10. Members grow in their gifts and talents.[6]

Our desire was to be a healthy, God-led church. We outlined our vision, purpose, and core values:

Our vision: To be a Christ-centered congregation joyfully growing in faith.

Our purpose: To love God by showing his love, proclaiming the Good News in Christ, being and making disciples for Him, and serving our neighbors.

Our core values:

- Our worship is sacramental and offered to the glory of God.
- We are theologically Anglican, and we interpret Scripture traditionally.
- Our greatest witness is lives transformed by and for God.
- We develop close personal relationships through Bible study, Christian fellowship, and prayer in small groups.
- We equip and empower lay people for ministry through biblically centered instruction and service.
- We demonstrate Jesus's compassion and ministry in the world through our outreach and pastoral care.[7]

Years later, the 2015 Vestry further defined All Saints by identifying five traits they saw among the members of our parish:

- We are a place of healing hospitality, a place of welcome and healing for those hurt or wounded.
- We see the church as family, where close relationships are formed and everyone is encouraged to participate.
- We are committed to spiritual formation in the Anglican way, forming people into the likeness of Christ within the three streams of Anglicanism: Scripture, Sacrament, and Spirit.
- All Saints has always had a heart for service, both inside the church and those outside, through vocation, community organizations, and global partners.
- All Saints has a history of being financially generous and responsible, budgeting according to what is pledged and giving at least 20 percent of our annual budget outside our church doors.[8]

Photo courtesy of All Saints Anglican Church

A group of parishioners enjoyed a church picnic on May 23, 2018.

Naming the *Crown*

With all the new and exciting things that were happening within our parish, it was necessary for us to have a newsletter. Kathy Herriman gladly took on the task of putting together our newsletters. Our first one, Volume 1, Issue 1, was published in March 2004 with the title "All Saints Anglican Church."

"When I was asked to compile the newsletter, I said 'sure,' without hesitation," Herriman commented in the first issue. "But the looks of empathy I have received from others make me wonder what I have gotten myself into. Nonetheless, I am excited about the prospect."[9]

Kathy asked that we submit our ideas for a name for our newsletter. A group got together and selected the *Crown*, the name submitted by Bob Hudson. The April 2004 newsletter was the first one with the new name. Our newsletter still bears that title today.

For many years, the *Crown* included things such as the abbreviated minutes from Vestry meetings. It was very common to see thank-you notes from parishioners who had been ministered to by the church in some special way, thank-you notes to parishioners who had served in various church events and/or outreach, updates on our ongoing outreach ministry, and reports from missionaries, just to name a few examples. Early issues of the *Crown* have been invaluable sources of information for me in the writing of this book, because it was a sort of journal that documented important things happening in our parish, especially in those early months and years.

In January 2005, after Kathy moved to Memphis, we hired Lindsey Young as a part-time staffer to prepare the Sunday church bulletins and the *Crown*. Lindsey remained in that capacity until she left in September 2005 to accept a teaching job. [10]

Fellowship

As a church family, All Saints has enjoyed many times of fellowship over the years. Aside from our Sunday worship services, we have had picnics. Our first one was May 14, 2004. [11]

We have also had Easter egg hunts, cookouts, campouts, fellowship dinners, Super Bowl parties, and blessing of the animals events.

On July 31, 2005, we began the first of many monthly Tell Out My Soul (TOMS) services, which were designed to be a time of "prayer, praise, music, witness, and Scripture." [12]

Pastorates were held often, usually twice a year, to give parishioners the opportunity to meet together in someone's home for study of a particular topic or book and to enjoy a meal. Pastorates were similar to our earlier small groups, but they met only

Photo courtesy of All Saints Anglican Church

Children take a break after an egg hunt on Easter Sunday, April 4, 2010.

Photo courtesy of All Saints Anglican Church

Fr. Chuck performs a blessing of the animals, October 4, 2008.

Photo courtesy of All Saints Anglican Church

A group of All Saints members come together for a men's gathering at the home of Chris and Judy Doyle, November 26, 2013.

about six times. The original small groups stayed together for years.

For a while, there were men's prayer and men's prayer-reunion groups that met weekly at the church for morning prayer. There was also a men's group that met periodically for a meal, usually a cookout, and fellowship. That gathering still happens today.

We had several Saints a la King gatherings in someone's home. Adults would be invited to come share a potluck meal and hear a special speaker. That later became known as Conversations a la Carte and still meets a few times each year.

CHAPTER EIGHT

Disciples for Christ

"I will put My Spirit within you
and cause you to walk in My statutes,
and you will keep My judgments and do them."

—Ezekiel 36:27, NKJV

Empowered by the Holy Spirit

So how did the Holy Spirit empower us? Through prayer, Bible study, and worship. Our Sunday worship services included traditional Anglican music and liturgy. There were Christian formation classes for children and adults and small groups that met regularly after our worship service.

After summer break, we celebrated Super Sunday to mark the beginning of new Christian formation classes. Our Christian Formation Committee included Courtney Davison, Linda Davenport, Harmony Sprinkle, Barbara Hudson, and Lynn Tatum. Some of our first teachers were Brad Box, Taylor Laird, Debbi Wagner, Sally Slack, Malcolm Pearson, John Herriman, and Jeff Garrety.[1]

Small Groups

We had four small groups that met weekly in members' homes to pray, study the Bible, and enjoy fellowship. We discussed concerns of the church and dedicated ourselves to becoming involved. Philippians 4:6 became the undergirding of our corporate prayer: "In everything, by prayer and supplication, with thanksgiving, let your requests be made known to God." Our first study, Rick Warren's *The Purpose Driven Life*, began during Lent. About 80 percent of the adults at All Saints were in small groups, whose hosts were Brad and Joanna Priester, Walter and Jane Townsend, Rich and Debbi Wagner, and Jim and Halina Warmbrod. Some groups lasted for years; the Townsend group remained active until 2016.

In her report to the Annual Parish Meeting in December 2004, Jane Garrety, as small group coordinator, described our purpose:

> Each gathering includes prayer, study, and fellowship. As we strengthen our friendship, we bear each other's burden and celebrate each other's victories. Together, we examine how we can walk closer with Christ. We accept and care for one another, forgive one another, encourage and build up one another, stimulate one another to love and do good deeds, pray for one another, serve one another, and love one another. [2]

I remember being in the Priesters' small group and meeting in their home in the Deepwood neighborhood. Their daughter, Halle, was about ten years old at the time and would stay upstairs during our prayer and Bible study times, but she would come down and join us for our fellowship time. Their dog, Chloe, however, wanted to be right in the middle of things and would join us for all of it. Joanna Priester remembers these meetings as being such sweet times. [3]

Priester remembers thinking how what we were doing at All

Photos courtesy of All Saints

ABOVE: Vacation Bible School ¡Fiesta! attendees, 2006, included Carole Beitz on the far left and Harmony Sprinkle at far right.

LEFT: Caroline Bagley and Jane Garrety prepare to sign in 2006 VBS attendees.

Saints was so new and how we could never have done what we did on our own; the Holy Spirit was our guide. We had strong leadership—both lay and clergy—and we found strength in our small numbers. She is grateful to Bishop Githiga and the Kenyan oversight that he so generously gave to us.[4]

Children's Ministries

We endeavored to be not just a child-friendly church but also a church that grows Christians. As early as January 2004, we had a plan for offering spiritual formation for our children and youth, ages nursery through twelfth grade. Noting that "our recent problems have been caused by a lack of knowledge of the Bible," [5] those involved with the children's program made concerted and deliberate efforts to offer Christian formation opportunities to encourage our children to become familiar with the Bible. Children's church gave our children the opportunity to learn all about "big church." They learned about the altar and why we have flowers, candles, and crosses. They learned to recite the twenty-third Psalm, the Nicene Creed, and the Lord's prayer, and how to add their own special prayers. [6]

Vacation Bible School became a yearly event; we would usually host forty to fifty participants. These included not only our parish children but also friends who came with them. The first year, we staged a "Serengeti Trek" from June 27-31, 2005. [7] In 2007, our VBS had almost fifty children participating, and over 90 percent of the church helped in some way. [8]

Youth Ministries

Our youth program was vibrant. Instrumental in keeping our youth program growing were Taylor Laird, Anne Rushing, and John Herriman. We formed a group of Young Anglican Christians (YACs). Led by Anne Rushing, they met weekly for fellowship and spiritual discussion. [9]

Rushing remembers our first Feast of Lights celebration on January 9, 2005, commemorating how the message of Jesus and His Gospel have advanced throughout the world and how the Church has grown since its earliest New Testament days. Dressed in costumes, the youth narrated and enacted milestones in the spread of Christianity. The service ended with the lighting of candles from person to person throughout the nave, as we each lit a candle from our neighbor, showing how we are to proclaim the Gospel to all the world. [10]

Periodically, there would be a Youth Sunday, with the youth leading our services. There would be a sermon by one of the youth,

Photo courtesy of All Saints Anglican Church

Youth meeting held in July 2009.

Photos courtesy of All Saints

ABOVE: Youths prepare for the Feast of Lights service, January 7, 2010. Pictured, left to right, are Lindy Tatum, Aiden Psungo, George Tatum, Daniel Pearson, Alex Carr, and Matthew Eans.

LEFT: Taylor Laird and Aiden Psungo prepare for a Christmas story performance in 2004.

and even a short children's sermon. Lectors, ushers, greeters, and acolyte roles would be filled by the youth. They would also read the prayers of the people, and the choristers and younger children would sing. The May 7, 2006, church bulletin lists the youth who participated in the youth service that day. Beth Herriman gave the sermon; lectors were Halle Priester and Andrew Wagner; ushers were Sara Slack and Roger Tatum; Wendy Googe was the cantor; the acolyte was Will Slack; Will Jones led the prayers of the people; and Matthew Eans, Ashton McGuire, Daniel Pearson, Frank Tatum, and Christian Wagner were the greeters.

In March 2009, All Saints youth partnered with the youth group at Faith Anglican Church in Cordova, Tennessee, to raise over $3,600 to support ten children in need for over a year. In May 2009, they held a second annual youth auction to raise funds for a mission trip to Standing Rock. That May, they participated in Project Acts, a week of community service and worship.[11]

Other youth events were Youthquake 2010, Christmas caroling, Super Bowl parties, and a Gumbo Fest in 2010 to finance their mission trip to Standing Rock.[12] Once, they joined the college group to go to a ropes course in Linden, Tennessee.[13]

Our first youth minister was Fr. Douglas Kimemia, who came to All Saints in 2005 but left in 2006 to work in full-time ministry and to continue theological studies at Memphis Theological Seminary. In October 2006, Fr. Chuck announced the hiring of a new youth minister, Brent Parrish, a junior at Union University, on a part-time basis.[14] When he left, Brian and Amanda Larsen Wells volunteered as youth ministers for a brief time after their children's ministry in Korea and before their move to Canada, where Brian would continue his education at McGill University.[15] There was a period when we were without a paid youth minister until Fr. Justin Baldwin served in that position from 2009-2011. He left All Saints to become a local pastor for Leeds UMC in Elkton, Maryland.[16]

After Fr. Baldwin's departure, another hiatus ensued. Fr. Wells returned and served as associate pastor to youth from 2013-2014 and then as priest to families from 2014-2021 before leaving All Saints to prepare for medical school.[17]

Adult Christian Formation

There were Christian formation opportunities for adults, too. In 2004, for example, two such classes were offered: Anglican Essentials and a Study of the Gospel of John. The Anglican Essentials class began with a study of the creeds, the authority of Scripture, and the Thirty-Nine Articles. This class was taught by Fr. Chuck, Rich Wagner, and Jeff Garrety. The Gospel of John class was led by Linda Hayes and Bob Hudson.[18]

As mentioned previously, Vestry members were assigned to ministries that reflected our spiritual gifts. We took our jobs seriously and endeavored to be Christ's disciples in carrying out those programs. We wanted to be the hands and feet of Jesus to serve not just our own people but also the mission field beyond our doors, as the sign we encounter upon leaving the church parking lot declares: "You are now entering the mission field."

Pastorates

All Saints began offering pastorates regularly in 2012. A pastorate is much like our earlier small groups. It is a small group of adults who meet for a brief time, usually once a week for five to six weeks, to share a potluck dinner and to discuss portions of Scripture or specific topics from a biblical perspective. Each pastorate has a leader and hosts, who offer their homes as meeting places. There are normally five or six pastorates that occur twice a year, in the spring and fall.

Stewardship

From our beginning, All Saints made stewardship a priority. As of February 25, 2004, All Saints had twenty-eight pledging units, representing approximately 75 percent of the total family units within our parish. Our pledges as of February 23, 2004, were $157,500. Pledges to our capital funds equaled $263,750. Contributions to date were $14,851.05 in the operating budget, $7,027 in the capital fund, and $1,595 in the memorial fund.[19]

Lloyd Tatum, in the March 2004 church newsletter, challenged all of us to review our stewardship pledges and ask, "Can't I do just a little bit more?" He added, "We are the shoulders upon which others are to stand. We are the sharp, pointed edge of the plow that digs just a little deeper so that the rest of the plow can do its work. History teaches us we will not be alone for long. Others will join us."[20]

Tatum was right! Several members took Tatum's challenge to "do a little bit more" and strengthened their commitments to our capital campaign. Carolyn Crowell committed to working an extra day each week so that she could contribute more.

Jane Garrety shared with me that Crowell's grandparents had been founding members of West Jackson Baptist Church. Crowell was proud that she, like her grandparents before her, had a part in the founding of a new church.[21] Barbara Hudson took on two extra piano students so she could contribute more. An anonymous person pledged six months' salary to stewardship.[22]

In December 2008, we paid off our mortgage. To celebrate, at the January 2009 Annual Parish Meeting, we burned the note in the parking lot. Later, we had a reception to celebrate this milestone.

As the Bible instructs us to tithe, we also tithe as a church. Ten percent of our budget was directed to outreach and 10 percent to the diocese. Today we give 12 percent of our budget to outreach.

Each stewardship season, which is in the fall, parishioners are asked to pledge portions of their time, talents, and finances to support the work of the church, based upon how the Holy Spirit is leading them. The budget is then set based on the amount that was pledged. We do not set a budget and then ask people to give toward that amount.

I Know the Plans I Have for You

Photo courtesy of All Saints Anglican Church

All Saints shares Bible study with the residents at Regency Retirement Village in 2015. Pictured are Fr. Wes, Caroline Bagley, Dian and Waring Hazlehurst, Rich Beitz, an unnamed Regency resident, Judy Rose, and Melinda Pearson, standing, and Jim Bagley, Carole Beitz, Harris Lake Smith, and Walter Townsend, seated.

Jim Warmbrod, in his capacity as stewardship chairperson, wrote in his report at the Annual Parish Meeting in 2004: "The emphasis [is] on Christian stewardship. Everything we have comes from God, and out of thanksgiving and love, we return a portion of that back to His Church for the work of the Church. It has nothing to do with the needs of All Saints Anglican Church. It is our need to show that thanksgiving and love. Besides treasure, it is our time and talent." [23]

Outreach/Serving Others

From the very beginning, All Saints has been involved in outreach ministry. The March 2005 issue of the *Crown* detailed a Missions/Ministry Fair, held on April 3, 2005, to inform our church community about the ministries and mission projects All Saints had committed to support.

Our ministry was widespread. For most of the years through 2013, All Saints was among the top five churches in the amount of money contributed in the "Walk for Life" at Birth Choice, which was quite remarkable, because we were ahead of large congregations like Englewood, Love and Truth, and Fellowship.[24] In addition, several of our members attended Birth Choice's annual fundraising banquet each spring.

Other ministries we served that first year, listed by Linda Davenport in her report to the Annual Parish Meeting in 2004, were the Regional Inter-Faith Association (RIFA) Community Kitchen; Gifts for the Christ Child, which we continue to support; Habitat for Humanity; the Heifer Project, which purchases farm animals for people in poorer countries; the Honduras mission; and missionaries Suzy McCall, Tillie Tiller, Horace Tipton, and Liz Hand.[25] All Saints parishioners also volunteered to man Salvation Army kettles for several Christmases.

Gretchen Filiatreau recalls the cowbell—bought by her mother in Switzerland and handed down to her—that would be rung at each Heifer gathering as the children and others would make their way to the chancel area to empty their miniature milk pails containing loose change into a large, genuine milk pail.[26]

Those first outreach committee members included Carolyn Crowell, Carlin Diffee, Gretchen Filiatreau, Jane Garrety, Rosie Grimball, Rezina Ham, Nelda Harrison, Shirley Phillips, Judy Rose, Anne Rushing, Harmony Sprinkle, Debbi Wagner, and Jim and Halina Warmbrod.[27]

Later outreach involvement has included helping people in Louisiana and Mississippi rebuild their farms; the RIFA school backpack program; Room in the Inn; monthly Bible studies with the residents at Regency Retirement Village; the American Red Cross; the Dream Center; Jackson Area Council on Alcoholism

Photo courtesy of All Saints Anglican Church

Dr. Ken Carr sees patients during the 2007 mission to Honduras.

and Drug Dependency's (JACOA's) prayer group; and WRAP. The Mary Magdalene ministry began as a fund to help women in need. Support for Area Relief Ministries (ARM), Court-Appointed Special Advocates (CASA), Church Planting Fund, ComeUnity Café, Lane College, and Union University's Homicide Walk came later.

Cornelia Tiller has volunteered for years at the Madison County Correctional Facility, where she shares the Gospel with female residents. She has acquired the nickname "Ms. Happy," because she always has a smile and spreads joy wherever she goes. In May 2023, she was honored by the Madison County Criminal Justice Center for her thirty years of service there. Their newly built visitation room was "dedicated in honor of Cornelia Tiller, affectionately known as 'Ms. Happy,' who has ministered in the name of Jesus to countless people that have walked these halls and lived behind these bars." [28]

Honduras Mission

Our biggest international outreach has always been our medical and construction ministry to Honduras. Dr. Jim Warmbrod started this ministry in 1998, when we were at St. Luke's.

Following the tornado in 2003, the Honduras mission went out one more time from St. Luke's before All Saints became the sending church.

The first mission that All Saints sponsored was June 3-12, 2004. Ten different parishes and churches were represented by those who traveled to Honduras that year. All Saints was represented by Warmbrod, Fr. Chuck, Dr. David Laird, George Davenport, Brad Box, and Bronson Doyle. [29] Warmbrod continued to sponsor yearly ministry opportunities after All Saints was formed. Even after he moved to Nashville in 2020, he has continued to lead our Honduras ministry.

Each year, in preparation for this ministry, the people of All Saints crowd together in our narthex for packing the pills that will be taken to Tegucigalpa, Honduras, and distributed to those who need them.

Pill-packing is a special ministry unto itself, because it gives all of us, young and old, the opportunity to feel as if we are a part of this mission.

What goes on behind the scenes, though, is what makes the process work. Jim Warmbrod collects medicine and supplies. Others—at first, it was Fr. Chuck and Bob Hudson—organize the actual pill-packing.

"Nobody knows how much work that takes," Fr. Chuck has said of the event. [30]

Other Outreach Ministries

All Saints has supported several missionaries over the years as well—Brian and Cindy Denker in Ethiopia, Jerry and Stacey Kramer in Tanzania and Iraq, Suzy McCall and Amanda Scott in Honduras, Craig Stewart in South Africa, Tillie Tiller in Chad, and Horace Tipton in Kenya.

Recent additions to our overseas ministry support are Fr. Herb

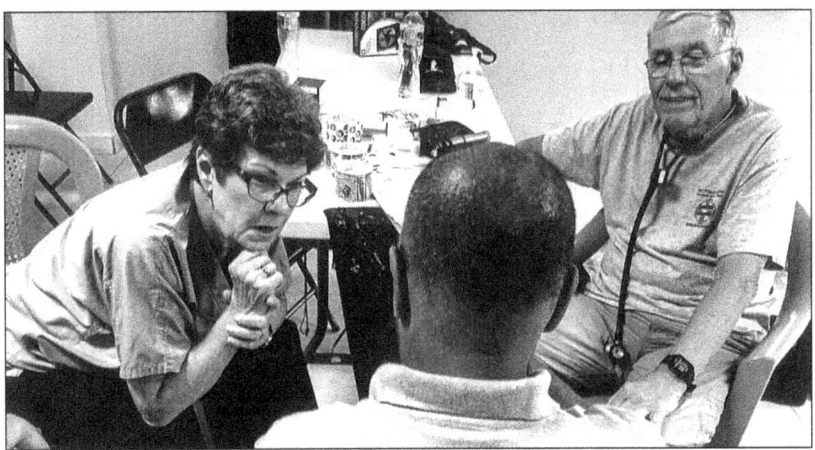

Photo courtesy of All Saints Anglican Church

Dr. Jim Warmbrod and Harriet Ross work with a patient during All Saints's 2018 mission to Honduras. Ross has served as an interpreter for our Honduras mission for many years.

Photo courtesy of All Saints Anglican Church

This Honduras pill-packing event was in 2018. Rita and Joe Davis III are in front. Others include Len Diffee, Celeste Pope, Ben Mehr, Greg Jordan, Chris Pope, Halina Warmbrod, Ron Marsh, and Fr. Chuck.

and Mary Hand in North Africa. The Lamb Institute in Honduras and the Warehouse in Cape Town are other international ministries All Saints has supported.

Most recently, All Saints Immigration Service (ASIS) was formed to assist immigrants with their various needs. See Chapter 13 for more information about this ministry.

CHAPTER NINE

Caring for Our Church Family

"... Let us do good to all, especially to those who are of the household of faith."

—Galatians 6:10, NKJV

Serving Our Own People

Pastoral Care

All Saints has always had a vibrant pastoral care ministry. This ministry has included not only taking meals to parishioners in times of illness, death, and birth but also making phone calls and visits, sending cards, and even providing transportation to church and for doctor visits.

A unique thing about this ministry is that its members are all the members of All Saints who provide care to other parishioners in times of need. It is a wonderful blessing to be on either the receiving or giving end of this ministry.

Kay Shearin currently oversees this ministry and keeps us updated with prayer requests and opportunities to reach out to our church family.

Morning Prayer

Several years ago, All Saints began morning prayer two days a week. That service has been extended to four mornings a week.

Critical Prayer Team

The critical prayer team was formed in the beginning as a way for us to report concerns that need immediate prayer. Requests were given to the coordinator, who then shared them with the team via text messaging. More recently, these critical prayer requests are sent via email. Many of us have benefited from this ministry.

Healing Prayer and Blessing Ministry

Terry Blakley credits Fr. Wes Gristy with starting the healing prayer and blessing ministry when he prayed for it as our new rector. For Blakley, her part in this ministry started around 2018 when she participated in a pastorate on fasting, led by Fr. Wes, and another one on healing prayer, led by Fr. Wes and Landon Preston. The Holy Spirit began to make her constantly hungrier for God.

One Sunday, Blakley heard Steven Swanson talking about a conference, "Deliver Us from Evil," being held at Falls Church (Virginia) Anglican Church. Blakley was able to attend.

From this conference came a feeling from the Holy Spirit that this was what God wanted All Saints to do. Blakley and her husband, Len Diffee, went to Fr. Wes and made a commitment to be available to offer healing prayers for those who needed them. She met with Fr. Wes often to discuss a healing prayer ministry.

Within a few months, several All Saints members attended a conference at Christian Healing Ministry in Jacksonville, Florida. Along with Blakley and Diffee, the group included Rob and Lynn Binkley, Caroljeanne Phillips, Ryan Pflasterer, and Steven Swanson. After this conference, Blakley began monthly healing prayer meetings for the team and for the church at large in August 2020.[1]

Blakley considers herself to be a foot soldier in this ministry.

"I may facilitate the host of dear people who pull into this ministry of prayer and blessing, but they are the real heroes!" she said. "Week in and week out, they labor with hearts of kindness, holiness, love, and the compassion of God. It is such a blessing for me to work alongside them all." [2]

The healing prayer team meets regularly with people from our church and our community. Team members commit to meet every week except the week of Thanksgiving, and the weeks before and after Christmas. This ministry is open to all, not just members of All Saints. Individual members of the team will make appointments to meet with others who cannot come on Tuesdays. Regular members are Terry Blakley and Len Diffee, Joyce Hefferman, Jordan Howerton, Paula Kirby, Ryan Pflasterer, Caroljeanne Phillips, Celeste Pope, and Sheila Williamson. There are mentors for the team. Fr. Chuck, for example, spoke to the team about how to pray for others and to have faith in their healing.

A prerequisite for being on the healing prayer team is training in the twenty-six healing miracles of Jesus. The team knows that it is only through love, mercy, and the Holy Spirit that any healing occurs. They don't do therapy or counseling, and they don't give advice. They listen, love, and pray through the power of the Holy Spirit for the person for whom they are interceding. Part of the healing prayer ministry is the blessing ministry for spiritual concerns such as marriage, children, burdens, and grieving.

Members of the prayer team who are called on for healing, blessing, and intercessory prayers are Olivia Abernathy, Jay and Katie Beavers, Rob and Lynn Binkley, Jane Garrety, Jordan Howerton, David and Taylor Laird, Joy Moore, Landon Preston, Frannie Smith, Nan Thomas, and Stephanie Traylor.

In the blessing service, there are liturgy and tangible elements. In each of the first two such services, participants and healing prayer team members were asked to write their burdens of sorrow, sin, or regret on a piece of paper and tie them around a rock. In one of these services, Fr. Wes took the rock from each person and prayed for each one's burden a blessing of relief and forgiveness. He told each person, "I am not giving this rock back to you." At that time, we were building the new nave, so he took all the rocks and buried them where the altar is. Fr. Chuck was there to bless the ceremony.

In everything they do, the healing prayer team looks to Fr. Wes for his guidance, knowledge, and approval. Fr. Wes said that when he first came to All Saints, he had prayed for two specific things: that All Saints would be a church-planting church and that it would be a church of healing prayer. Fr. Wes has always been joyful, open, and encouraging with Blakley and the team. [3]

The newest part of the prayer ministry is The Blessing Place at The Mission Abbey. Blakley described it in this way: "We seek to take the lovely presence of Christ to people in all walks of life in our community to bless them through acts of love and kindness." [4] This ministry was commissioned by Fr. Wes on May 19, 2024.

Out of The Blessing Place has emerged a Blessing Blast, which comes totally from the Holy Spirit. Team members meet monthly to ask the Holy Spirit to lead them to people who need their ministry immediately.

They work in pairs, which reminds me of Jesus sending out his disciples "two by two." (See Mark 6:7.) The Holy Spirit leads them to a place where they bless all who work there—staffs at nursing homes and service organizations, businesses and their staffs, restaurants and their servers, and even to a dump site where they prayed for the man in charge.

They always take something tangible, like flowers or donuts. They go wherever God leads them, and they never know ahead of time where that will lead. They ask for permission to distribute the gifts and ask the workers individually for permission to say a prayer or blessing over them. So far, no one has refused them, and people have been genuinely touched by the acts of kindness.

The team is experiencing so much joy in ministering to

Photo courtesy of All Saints Anglican Church

All Saints women gather at a Ladies Koinonia meeting to enjoy fellowship and prayer, July 9, 2018.

strangers that the Blessing Blast often splashes back on them![5]

Blakley added that God honored Fr. Wes in bringing to life his vision of All Saints becoming a church of prayer and blessing, which has become like a field of flowers in which we get to run![6]

Silent Retreats

Before she was even ordained, Deacon Nan Thomas began offering silent retreats three or four times a year. These retreats are always on Saturdays from eight thirty to eleven thirty in the morning. They offer special opportunities to be with God in silence and solitude. "Taking time apart calls us into a different frame of mind—a different way of being with God. . . . We intentionally fix our eyes on Jesus to be with him."[7]

Ladies Koinonia

Sheila Williamson hosts the monthly Ladies Koinonia

meetings, where the women of All Saints meet for fellowship and prayer. They sometimes have book studies; one recent book study was Jim Wilder's *Joyful Journey*, a book recommended by Bishop Atwood.

Sunday Ministries
Fellowship/Hospitality Ministry

In the beginning, this team was headed by Linda Hayes. In her report at the December 2004 Annual Parish Meeting, she thanked Joanna Priester, her co-chair, and Jane Townsend and Shirley Phillips for their faithful service to the team. Our last fellowship of that year was a Bring-a-Leftover-Christmas-Goody-to-Share reception held on December 26, following our service of Lessons and Carols. [8]

Since that time, volunteers have always worked behind the scenes, taking care of things without seeking any recognition. We have always relied on Lupe Mitchell for her beautiful, delicious cakes for special events, especially Easter. She has also provided tasty hors d'oeuvres for the many receptions we have had over the years. Celeste Pope oversees the Sunday morning refreshments that are enjoyed each week. She is assisted regularly by several other volunteers, including Kay Shearin, Vicki Burch, Joyce Hefferman, and Loyanne Cope. Others assist her periodically, including nine-year-old Anne Claire Abernathy. [9]

Music Ministry

Our first pianist/choirmaster was Joanie Forbes, who had come with us from St. Luke's. She is a very accomplished musician who had played piano and organ for several Anglican parishes, including St. George's and St. Paul's Episcopal churches in Dayton, Ohio. She had also worked with Wright State University and the Dayton Opera before she came to St. Luke's and, ultimately, to All Saints. [10] Gretchen Filiatreau recalls that Forbes's musical ability, historical

Photo courtesy of Judy Rose

Joanie Forbes, wearing blue, chats with parishioners at a reception in her honor in 2008. Also pictured is Andy Hudson in the green shirt.

knowledge, sense of humor, volunteer spirit with no salary, endless hours of work, and devotion to the church had a great deal to do with enriching the new church. The choir was always ready to sing at all services, weddings, funerals, and any occasion when music was needed, especially to create a base for congregational singing.[11]

In her report to the Annual Parish Meeting in December 2004, Forbes recalled our beginnings:

"2004 has been an exciting year, our first for the choir of All Saints.... We cannot help but think back on all the blessings we have received from our Heavenly Father. Almost immediately, the board authorized the purchase of choir vestments.... Imagine my surprise when I found out the Almy Company was having a special promotion for the state of Tennessee, 25 percent off! Now we looked like a choir. ... We needed to sound like a choir, and to accomplish this, we needed real music.... Gifts, memorial donations, and now a budget allowed me to shop. This occurred right before the yearly music sales, allowing us to get some favorite anthems, some with a savings of 32 percent. We now have the beginnings of a music library."[12]

Forbes also commented on the chime bars donated by the Hudsons, saying that they not only added an Anglican touch to our service, "they also keep us in tune!" [13]

Forbes and her husband, John, hosted the first Choir and Friends party on September 1, 2004. The "friends" invited that year were the retired board and the new Vestry. The choir wanted to thank them for giving "so much so that there could be an All Saints." [14]

Forbes had been our pianist/choirmaster since the very beginning. It was sad for us, especially for members of the choir, when she announced in 2008 that she and her husband, a nurse anesthetist, would be moving to Mt. Juliet, Tennessee, when he retired from Jackson-Madison County General Hospital.

"Not a day goes by that I don't think of Jackson and All Saints," Forbes wrote years later. "It was hard to leave. This was the first parish I ever played for without pay, but I gained more by giving back. Judy Rose has sent several pictures of the newer All Saints. I love the tower, and the stonework is so nice. I sat and studied it and thought that I had been a part of that church's beginning. Even though I played only a tiny part, perhaps my efforts may have helped things along the way. It is a wonderful newer parish, which made me realize that God does move in mysterious ways." [15]

Dr. Randall Bush, a Union University professor, became our new pianist/choirmaster. He served us until sometime in 2012.

In 2012, we moved to two services, with the choir singing traditional music at the first service, accompanied by Dr. Bush at the piano. A different choir, accompanied by Amanda Larsen Wells on guitar, sang contemporary music at the second service.

After Dr. Bush left, Bev Carr became our pianist and served until 2013. Like Joanie Forbes, she declined to be paid for her service to All Saints.

When Fr. Chuck approached Carr about becoming our pianist in 2012, she agreed but told him that he must look for someone else, because she was not up to the task and not the one to do this. She said that All Saints, both the choir and the congregation, deserved better. But her love for All Saints and her desire to step up when needed entered into her decision to say yes. After Easter 2013, Carr went to Fr. Chuck and again reiterated that he needed to be looking for someone else to be in charge of the music program. She had been disappointed with her performance at Easter and felt that she was not what All Saints needed. She continued to play for us until Dr. Tang came in the summer of 2013. Carr told me that she was unaware of the visit Dr. Tang made to All Saints before he was hired. She told him later that it was a good thing that she didn't know he was there or she might have passed out on the spot! [16]

The choir was happy to have Carr as our pianist. She was dedicated to the job, driving an hour from her home in Martin to get to the church early on Sunday mornings so the choir could rehearse the music for the worship service that day. Since it was such a long drive for her, we didn't expect her to come in the middle of the week for rehearsal. Thankfully, Forbes had left a well-stocked music library, so we sang anthems we already knew.

In May 2013, Dr. Jordan Tang was looking for a music position. His daughter, Paige, told him that someone had announced at a student recital at Union University that there was an opening at All Saints. He called Fr. Chuck to learn more. [17]

Gretchen Filiatreau recalls that one day Fr. Chuck came home grinning and asked her, "Guess who came to see me today?"

After many wrong guesses, she gave up and asked, "Who?"

"Jordan Tang," he answered. Her reaction? There was great whooping and hollering.

"What did he want? Does he want to join us? Tell me! Tell me!" she demanded.

"He wants to go to work," Fr. Chuck said.

"Hire him! Hire him! Tie him to the piano before he changes his mind!" she said. She could not believe their good fortune. [18]

Dr. Tang interviewed with Fr. Chuck in May. It was the easiest job interview he had ever done. When Dr. Tang asked, "When do I start?" Fr. Chuck replied, "How about July 1?" Dr. Tang said the timing couldn't have been better; his contract with the Jackson Symphony ended June 30. Fr. Chuck didn't know this fact at the time, but God did, and He intervened. Dr. Tang and his wife, Cindy, visited All Saints in June. He first met with the choir in June.[19]

Prior to his coming to All Saints, Dr. Tang had served for twenty-seven years as music director of the Jackson Symphony and twenty-three years with the Paducah Symphony. He has also served as an associate conductor of the Charlotte Symphony. He has been a guest conductor for several other symphonies and is an accomplished composer and arranger.

His education includes degrees from the Chinese University of Hong Kong, Wittenberg University, the Cleveland Institute of Music, and the University of Utah.

I asked Dr. Tang if it was hard for him to get used to our traditional Anglican music. He said that he had had some experience with music in a liturgical format and that the structure and liturgy of the Anglican church made it much easier to determine which hymns would be sung each Sunday. He looked at some of our old church bulletins to see what things we had been doing. His first impression was that our choir was small but knowledgeable about music.[20]

Dr. Tang started our tradition of having a string quartet accompany us on Easter Sunday and Christmas Eve. This makes those days even more festive and joyful than they already are. The choir always looks forward to the refreshments provided by Dr. Tang and his wife, Cindy, preceding the Christmas Eve service. Since choir rehearsal usually begins around seven thirty in the evening for the ten o'clock service, these refreshments are most welcome!

On July 1, 2023, Dr. Tang achieved the milestone of ten years of music ministry at All Saints. Unfortunately, we forgot and let that special day go by unnoticed. It wasn't until September that we realized our faux pas, and on September 24, 2023, we belatedly

I Know the Plans I Have for You

Photo courtesy of All Saints Anglican Church

Music director Dr. Jordan Tang performs during Bishop Atwood's visit, November 6, 2016.

celebrated his ministry with a cake after each service that day.

For several years, we had a Lessons and Carols service the Sunday after Christmas. These services were designed to let us sing all the carols we couldn't sing during Advent and Christmas.[21]

Becky Googe initiated a chorister's group in 2005. She had been involved in this ministry at St. Luke's, so it was only fitting that she should continue providing a venue for our elementary school-age children (second grade to fifth or sixth grade) who loved to sing. Becky told me that Fr. Chuck's plan was to have the choristers sing four times a year during the Sunday morning service. Becky usually had them sing once in every liturgical season that coincided with the academic school year. They sang during Advent, during the family Christmas service on Christmas Eve, for the Feast of Lights service, on Palm Sunday, and on Youth Sunday. Over the few years that the chorister group existed, members included, at various times, George and Lindy Tatum, Ricardo and Aiden Psungo, Anna Caroline and Miles Moore, Clare Sprinkle, Ashley Arinze, Weston and Jenna Box, and Wendy Googe.[22]

In her report to the Annual Parish Meeting in 2008, Becky shared that the group of choristers now numbered eight children. She also reported that Ricardo Psungo, our oldest male chorister at the time, chose to continue singing with the group despite the fact that he had "graduated" from elementary. Wendy Googe continued to sing with the choir long after her elementary years, too, even through high school. She lent moral support to the younger children and helped them get over the stage fright of singing in church. [23]

Altar Guild

The altar guild is a ministry that works behind the scenes to ensure that the altar is prepared for any service where Holy Eucharist is celebrated. That includes Sunday mornings and special services like Christmas Eve and some weddings and funerals. The people involved in this ministry prepare the altar for worship each Sunday, coming on Saturday to lay out utensils and elements needed for Eucharist. They are also responsible for washing service vessels and laundering altar linens. They polish silver altar furnishings monthly. It's not just a Sunday morning commitment.

The altar guild has three teams who rotate their duties throughout the year. There are three leaders, Marty Courcelle, Judy Rose, and Stephanie Traylor, and assistants for those teams, Loyanne Cope, Katie Howerton, Denise Matthews, and Lynn Tatum.

Marty Courcelle was on the altar guild at St. Luke's, and she continued that ministry at All Saints, along with Linda Hayes, who had also been on St. Luke's altar guild. Courcelle is now the altar guild coordinator. At first, it was just Courcelle and Hayes, and they carried the altar furnishings and utensils in a cardboard box, which they dubbed the "traveling sacristy," to and from our early meetings with the Townsends and Warmbrods, keeping the supplies, linens, and utensils in their homes between meetings.

Hayes made the first veil for our altar. The veil is the piece of fabric over cardboard that covers the chalice and paten on the altar.

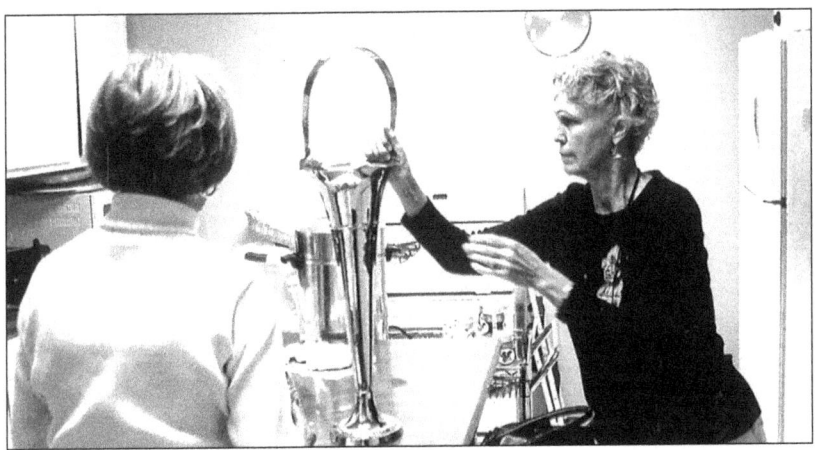

Photo courtesy of All Saints Anglican Church

Marty Courcelle, right, and Ruth Oliver clean the silver altar vases for Christmas 2009.

Courcelle said that the hardest part of her job as coordinator is to find people willing to commit to this ministry and to stay with it long enough to learn the job well.[24]

Denise Matthews, a member of the altar guild, made more altar linens—even a fair linen, the large white covering for the altar table. The old ones are twenty years old and are beginning to show their age. Also, we now share our altar linens with Mission St. James, so we need to have more on hand.[25] Matthews has made coverings for the new kneelers we will use when we go to the altar for communion in the new nave.

See the Appendix for notes on the meaning behind every aspect of the altar.

Flower Guild

Since the beginning, Fr. Chuck has overseen the arranging of the floral adornments that have graced our altar for special occasions such as Easter and services. Many of us have observed over the years that had he not been ordained as a priest, he could have had a successful career as a florist. He is that good!

Over the years, many people have volunteered to help Fr. Chuck decorate. In the early years, Sally Slack, Caroline Bagley, Dian Hazlehurst, and Carlin Diffee helped. More recently, volunteers have included Sally Slack, Melisande Rowe, Lynn Binkley, Joanna Priester, Vicki Burch, Cindy Jayne, Grace Ann House, Franny Smith, and Carl Diffee.[26]

New Members

In his report to the Annual Parish Meeting in 2004, John Herriman reminded us that we had started as a core group of around forty-five people and had grown to about one hundred attending church each Sunday. One of the goals of the new member ministry was to "actively seek out and bring into the church those in our community who do not have a church home." He thanked Bill Boggs, Walter Townsend, and Billy Slack for assisting him.

He reported that ushers and greeters had a large part in welcoming newcomers each Sunday. He mentioned Lou and Marty Courcelle, Kathy Herriman, Rich and Debbi Wagner, Jeff and Rezina Ham, Charles Richards, Joe Davis, Bettye Sullivan, Katie Herriman, Jim and Halina Warmbrod, and Kenny and Sarah Beth Hanson in particular.[27]

Lectors

In the beginning, Charles Richards coordinated the lector ministry. In his report to the Annual Parish Meeting in 2004, he listed those who were serving in this ministry: Jim Bagley, Michael and K. P. Collier, George Davenport, Jeff Garrety, Sarah Beth Hanson, John and Kathy Herriman, Bob and Barbara Hudson, Charles Richards, Anne Rushing, Bettye Sullivan, Rich Wagner, and Halina Warmbrod.[28] Richards himself is an extraordinary lector, with just the right voice and diction for us to understand him wherever we are sitting in the nave.

CHAPTER TEN

Rejoice in the Lord Always

> "Rejoice in the Lord always.
> Again I will say, rejoice!"
> —Philippians 4:4, NKJV

Milestones and Changes

We did rejoice in the Lord, and it must have shown. In February 2012, Fr. Ron McCrary stayed with the Filiatreaus for three days while he conducted what Gretchen recalls was a church survey for the International Diocese. He interviewed every group and almost every parishioner at All Saints. Gretchen remembers that he was surprised to find "happiness and an absence of conflict." He said, "This is unusual, and I haven't found it in other churches I've visited." [1]

McCrary did make two recommendations:

1. Take down the name tag board in the front hall and have pens and temporary name tags on a table for everyone to make their own every Sunday. This will prevent visitors from feeling different from members, because they will all have the same kind of tag.

2. Move to two services. His reasoning was that people feel cramped and don't like to sit too close to others. "Ironically," Gretchen recalls, "after all this talk about the absence of strife, this second recommendation led to the first incidence of real strife." [2] More about that later.

In Times of Celebration
All Saints "Firsts"

All Saints has enjoyed several joyful milestones over the years. The first All Saints baby was Lydia Jane Sprinkle, born to Don and Harmony Sprinkle on August 23, 2004. [3] The first couple to be married at All Saints were Katie Herriman and Ray Rhody on May 27, 2006. [4] The first person baptized at All Saints was Brandon Miles Moore, son of Brandon and Beth Moore, and grandson of Jim and Caroline Bagley, on Easter Eve, April 15, 2006. [5]

On August 28, 2005, Bishop Githiga confirmed our first confirmands at All Saints: Rich and Carole Beitz, Wendy Googe, Katie Jones, Will Jones, Lynn Tisdale, Andrew Wagner, Kali Wagner, and Blake Williams. As of November 2023, there have been 234 confirmations at All Saints. [6]

The first funeral held at All Saints was for Prissy Maness, daughter of Lupe Mitchell, who died on April 7, 2007. [7]

A New Diocese and a New Bishop

In 2009, the International Diocese was a founding member of the Anglican Church in North America (ACNA), and the Rt. Rev. Dr. Bill Atwood was its first bishop. He was an Air Force pilot before entering the ministry. In 2000, he left parish ministry to serve as general secretary of the Ekklesia Society. In 2006, he formally left ECUSA in his stand for traditional Anglicanism in America. When he was elected bishop in the Anglican Church, more archbishops participated in his consecration than any other in American history. In 2009, he became diocesan bishop in the

I Know the Plans I Have for You

Photo courtesy of All Saints Anglican Church
Bishop Atwood visits with the children, January 29, 2018.

ACNA. He served as suffragan bishop of All Saints Cathedral Diocese in the Anglican Church of Kenya (ACK). He also served as the ambassador for the Fellowship of Confessing Anglicans (also known as GAFCON).[8]

All Saints became a member of the ACNA in 2009. How this province began was clearly a working of the Holy Spirit and an answer to prayer.

ACNA was formed out of the Global Anglican Fellowship Conference (GAFCON), a worldwide family of Anglicans whose purpose is to keep and restore the Bible to the heart of the Anglican Communion. GAFCON officially began in 2008, but the journey toward its birth began in February 1997, in Kuala Lumpur, during the Second Encounter of the Global South Anglican Communion. It was during this conference that "a statement was issued expressing concern about the apparent setting aside of the biblical teaching by some provinces and dioceses." This statement called for a dialogue in a spirit of unity before any part of the Anglican

Communion began any "radical changes to Church discipline and moral teaching."[9] Unfortunately, this plea, along with several similar warnings, was largely ignored.

Ten years later, in February 2007, a meeting of the primates of the Anglican Communion was held in Tanzania. At this meeting, the primates experienced an "agonizing time as they tried to repair the Communion that had been so badly broken."

Their earlier prediction, in a 2003 primates' meeting, "that rejection of the faith committed to us would 'tear the fabric of our Communion at its deepest level,' has proved to be accurate." In one last attempt to restore unity, they proposed a period of seven months for those who had brought the Communion "to the brink of destruction" to reconsider their actions and to stop those who had "polarized our beloved church."[10] The September 30, 2007, deadline they set for receiving an answer was ignored. They concluded that:

> There is no longer any hope, therefore, for a unified Communion. The intransigence of those who reject biblical authority continues to obstruct our mission, and it now seems that the communion is being forced to choose between following their innovations or continue on the path that the Church has followed since the time of the Apostles. We have made enormous efforts since 1997 in seeking to avoid this crisis, but without success. Now we confront a moment of decision. If we fail to act, we risk leading millions of people away from the faith revealed in the Holy Scriptures and also, even more seriously, we face the real possibility of denying our Saviour, the Lord Jesus Christ.[11]

Several things were at stake: (1) the struggle over authority,

I Know the Plans I Have for You

for the Church, and for the Christian; (2) the struggle over the interpretation of Scripture; (3) the struggle over theological pluralism in the Church; (4) the struggle over the understanding of mission; and (5) the struggle over post-colonial power relationships.[12] In his comments over what was at stake, Jeff Garrety pointed out that All Saints almost immediately began small group Bible studies as a result of the second issue.[13]

In June 2008, GAFCON held its first conference in Jerusalem. Garrety was among the attendees. When asked what was his prayer for GAFCON, he replied, "My hope is that there will be one orthodox province in North America. [GAFCON is a] real rescue effort coming from primates of other provinces."[14] As we now know, Garrety's hope was realized with the formation of the ACNA.

On March 29, 2009, the Vestry approved a resolution to "affirm and subscribe to the Constitution and Canons of the Anglican Church in North America."[15]

A New Rector

On March 27, 2009, Fr. Chuck Filiatreau celebrated the fortieth anniversary of his ordination to the priesthood.

"All Saints planned a surprise celebration on Palm Sunday, April 5, inviting family and friends from Arkansas where Fr. Chuck had been a priest from 1968-1990," Gretchen Filiatreau recalled. "It was a most special reunion for all of us."[16]

In his letter of invitation to the event, Rich Wagner wrote:

> We have all felt his caring touch. Time has not slowed him down. Today, for example, he preached the sermon, celebrated the Eucharist, visited the sick at the hospital, and attended our confirmation classes. He has performed our marriages and baptisms, comforted the hurting and sick, and buried our loved ones. Countless sermons and

Vestry meetings have not dulled his selfless spirit or his sense of humor. He still does practical things, too, like shoveling snow. Chuck is always there.[17]

Gretchen commented that she would add to Rich's list:

> ... cleans bathrooms, cleans houses, mops, sweeps, moves furniture, helps with the soup kitchen and Salvation Army kettles, carries Holy Communion to homes and nursing homes, feeds ducks, conducts youth group, joins youth for a ropes course and canoe trips, visits prison, serves as hospital chaplain sometimes in the middle of the night, does children's sermons, Bible studies, and counseling, sets up for pill packing, made fifteen trips on the Honduras mission and once pulled thirty teeth after a dentist taught him how, made several trips to Africa to visit our bishop, and decorates the church with flowers at Christmas and Easter.[18]

Fr. Chuck had announced his intentions to retire as our rector when he reached the age of seventy-two, which would happen in 2014. We didn't want to think about that, but we knew we would abide by his wishes. We were happy for Gretchen and him, but it was a bittersweet time for the parish. They knew they would remain at All Saints, but they deliberately stayed away for a period of six months to give the new rector a time to bond with us without the distraction of having the retired rector in attendance each Sunday.

Fr. Chuck's retirement party was in late June 2014. He left town about three days later on a bicycle trip through Portugal. When he returned, he and Gretchen visited a different church every Sunday until Christmas.[19]

I Know the Plans I Have for You

Photo courtesy of All Saints Anglican Church

This 2019 photo shows the Gristy family: Abbie, Fr. Wes, Weston (back), and Lawson and Natalie (front).

In 2011, the Rev. Wes Gristy had left Fellowship Bible Church, where he had served as community pastor. His leaving had not been a pleasant experience for him and his family, and they struggled with questions about their future. Fr. Chuck knew Wes had left Fellowship and reached out to him and Abbie. Jonathan Stewart, who had previously attended Fellowship before coming to All Saints, encouraged them to visit All Saints. They met with Rich and Debbi Wagner in the Wagner home for discussion and later attended inquirers' classes.

Wes and Abbie weren't exploring just Anglicanism; they visited several churches over a period of three or four months. The only thing Wes and Abbie had previously known about Anglicanism in Jackson was that there was an Anglican church on McClellan Road that they used to drive past on their way to USJ, which is where Fellowship's members met before they built at their current location.

Wes and Abbie's first impression of Anglicanism was that it was very weird. But they found that the people at All Saints were incredibly warm and hospitable. Things became clearer when they attended their first instructed Eucharist, led by Nathan Shelby. Fr. Wes said it felt like coming home again after twelve years in the Disciples of Christ church and then later in the Baptist church, too. They discovered that Anglicanism, like the Disciples of Christ churches, was liturgical, and they were excited about the traditions in the Anglican church.[20]

Fr. Wes and Abbie felt they needed to share with those who loved and prayed for them a "thoughtful explanation" of why they made the decision to become Anglicans. Their decision was based on several factors that strongly appealed to them and caused them to move in that direction.

In a paper, "The Appeal of Anglicanism," they identified six factors that stood out, which I have summarized:

- **The Anglican communion:** The heritage of Anglicanism reaches all the way back to the early church. It is a global community consisting of over eighty million members worldwide, making it the third largest Christian communion in the world.
- **Anglican worship:** Anglicans are united in their worship more than almost anything else by the Book of Common Prayer. In each province around the world, we all share with other Anglicans on a daily, weekly, and yearly basis.

Anglican worship is a participatory experience. Among other things, we pray aloud together, we recite the creeds together, we confess our sins together, and we receive communion together.

Jesus Christ is the center of the worship experience. In every Anglican worship service Fr. Wes and Abbie attended, the table and the cross stood front and center. The sermon is only one of many parts of a worship service, and music leaders are off to one side so as not to distract worshipers from Jesus Christ.

- **Anglican theology:** The Thirty-Nine Articles of Religion is the historically defining statement of doctrines for the Church of England and the Anglican Church worldwide. Anglicanism stresses Scripture as the final authority for matters of belief and practice. Tradition and reason also play key roles in Anglican theology, but they are never placed on equal footing with the Bible as a norm of faith. Anglicanism is historically orthodox in affirming key doctrines such as the Trinity, the deity of Christ, the incarnation, and the resurrection.

- **The Anglican attitude:** The spirit of Anglicanism is often described as having "a sweet reasonableness" toward other Anglicans, other believers, and unbelievers alike. Anglicans deeply value their own tradition, but they do not think of themselves as the one and only true church. The Lord's table is always open to every baptized believer of Jesus.

- **Church leadership:** The vision and structure of leadership in the Anglican Church is one of the most attractive things about Anglicanism. The leadership structure is arranged with a number of checks and balances. A bishop provides pastoral oversight and guidance to a group of churches (a diocese); a priest is given latitude in guiding a local church to live out its mission; and the priest works with a Vestry, parishioners elected by the congregation, to make administrative and budget decisions.

- **The mission of the Church:** Anglicans believe that God works through the Church to bring all things under the reign of Jesus Christ. Central to this task is making disciples who are transformed by the power of the Spirit to be a life-giving body of God's grace and healing. The mission of the Church is holistic, centered on the Gospel, and carried forth by local church communities empowered by the Spirit.[21]

(Note: Fr. Wes includes the points made in this paper in our Discover All Saints class.)

Fr. Wes received a bachelor's degree in religion from Wayland Baptist University in Plainville, Texas, in 1999. He received a master of theology degree in New Testament Studies and Pastoral Leadership from Dallas Theological Seminary in 2005. He began his work in ministry as college and singles pastor at First Baptist Church in Cedarville, Texas, from 2000-2005, while he was still a seminary student.

He served at Fellowship Bible Church in Jackson from 2005-2011, first as equipping pastor and later as community pastor. [22] Fr. Wes was ordained to the diaconate in 2012 [23] and to the priesthood in the Anglican Church in 2013. [24] He became associate pastor for programs in 2012, co-rector in 2014, and was installed as rector of All Saints on August 24, 2014. [25]

Fifteenth Anniversary Celebration

On Sunday, February 17, 2019, fifteen years and two days after we first worshiped together at our "old building" at 212 McClellan Road, we celebrated our fifteenth anniversary as a church. The bulletin cover for that special service shows a picture of our first bulletin as a church, dated February 15, 2004.

We sang the same hymns and listened to the same lectionary readings from our first service.

In contrast, that day's bulletin was thirty-two pages long, while the first-ever All Saints bulletin filled all of four pages! Fr. Brian Larsen Wells preached the sermon, the choral anthem was "The Lord Is My Light," and the altar flowers were given "to the glory of God" by All Saints' parishioners. [26]

In Times of Adversity
Our 'Flood'

As Christians, we are taught to give thanks to God in every situation and to realize that adversity usually leads us to something better when we allow it to do so.

One of those adverse periods was the flooding of our church in 2010.

Saturday, January 9, was a cold day, and as I walked into the church to prepare the altar for the next day's Eucharist, I realized I was walking in about two inches of water.

A water pipe in the ceiling above Fr. Chuck's office had frozen and burst, and water was everywhere. I called Fr. Chuck and described the situation, and he immediately called Brad Box, who lived nearby, and had him rush to the church and turn off the water at the outside meter.

Soon after Box arrived on the scene, Fr. Chuck appeared. By that time, other parishioners had been called, and people started showing up at the church to see what needed to be done and to help wherever they could.

Water covered the floors in the narthex, kitchen, and some of the children's area, and was about halfway down into the nave. Bronson Doyle, who oversaw the property at that time, supervised the cleanup and was "an invaluable resource," Fr. Chuck recalled.[27]

It was clear that we wouldn't be able to have services at All Saints the next day, so Fr. Chuck contacted the clergy at Fellowship Bible Church. After explaining our predicament, he asked if we could use their barn for worship for a few Sundays until repairs could be made. The clergy graciously agreed, much as the ministry at Englewood had done in 2004 when they allowed us to use the Old English Inn.

The carpet in the nave was ruined and had to be replaced, as did the other flooring and baseboards in all the areas where the floor had been under water.

The greatest damage, though, was to Fr. Chuck's office. Most of his books were damaged or destroyed, and efforts to salvage the damaged ones were futile. Fr. Chuck remarked that he was still able to access many of the books online, but some of the destroyed books had special meaning other than the text they contained.

We met at Fellowship's barn for about a month while repairs were made. We took vestments and worship paraphernalia along with altar supplies for Eucharist and stored them in a closet at the barn so we wouldn't have to carry them back and forth each week. There was a large, open space that we could use as our nave and a stage that we used as an altar. There were plenty of chairs, a keyboard, a lectern, and even microphones. There were also restrooms and a kitchen, so we could easily prepare and clean up after Eucharist.

Despite the damage and inconvenience the flood had caused, we were filled with gratitude that God had once again provided a place for us, as He had before. He blessed us with willing Christian friends who graciously allowed us to use their facilities.

After we were finally able to return to our building, Fr. Chuck encouraged us to contact members of Fellowship and express gratitude for their generosity, and many of us did. The March 2010 issue of the *Crown* reported a request to the Vestry that we buy a coat rack for Fellowship's barn in appreciation for what they had done for us. [28]

Choir Disharmony

In 2012, we moved to two services, with the choir singing at both. This led to the real strife mentioned earlier in this chapter. Choir members disagreed about what kind of music we should be singing in church. Should we continue with traditional Anglican music or should we change to contemporary praise music, which had become a popular trend in many churches in Jackson and elsewhere? There were strong opinions for both alternatives.

Fr. Chuck met with the choir and asked us to share our thoughts about what should be done. A compromise was reached when it was decided that one service would offer traditional music, accompanied by Dr. Bush on piano, and the other one would have contemporary praise music, accompanied by Amanda Larsen

Wells on guitar. We were encouraged to sing in both services as a show of unity and goodwill, but that didn't happen. Most of us chose to sing at only the service that offered the music we preferred, but a couple of us continued to sing in both services.

After a trial period of approximately two months, it was becoming obvious that this arrangement was causing more disunity, not only within the choir, but also within the church as a whole. Fr. Chuck decided we would return to our traditional music, which was so much a part of Anglican worship, for both services. A few people had their feelings hurt, but in the end, most of us realized that Fr. Chuck had made the right decision for the benefit of our fellowship at All Saints.

COVID

In early 2020, the COVID pandemic hit and made it necessary for All Saints to cancel services for two weeks. After that, services resumed, but we were required to wear masks. Many of us resumed attending weekly services; however, others chose not to attend so long as mask-wearing was mandatory. During the time of mandatory mask-wearing, those who did not attend church in person were able to access services via Zoom. (Although we are now post-COVID, services are still available on Zoom.)

After a few months, we could remove our masks when sitting or standing, but we had to use them when moving around. Eventually, masks became optional.

More Water Damage

In January 2023, thirteen years after our first frozen pipes, a water pipe in the foyer ceiling just outside the nave froze and burst. All Saints was again looking at a major disruption to our services and activities.

This time, though, the damage wasn't as severe as it had been in 2010. We were able to minimize the damage by immediately using large fans to begin drying the floors. The flooring and carpeting were saved, and we did not have to replace those. The major disruption was not being able to use the water in the kitchen until the burst pipes could be repaired.

For almost a month, members of the altar guild had to get water from the ladies' restroom to prepare and clean up the altar for Sunday services. The hospitality committee had to do the same when they provided refreshments each week. A church-wide dinner that had been scheduled during that time was still able to occur, even though the caterers, too, had to get water from the women's restroom. We were thankful that the damage wasn't more extensive than it was and that things were back to normal relatively soon.

PART FOUR:
Hope and a Future

"'For I know the plans I have for you,'
declares the Lord,
'plans to prosper you and not to harm you,
plans to give you hope and a future.'"

—Jeremiah 29:11, NIV

CHAPTER ELEVEN

Mission Abbey

"Together we are forming a community that is responsive to God's Spirit, a community that God has brought to this unique moment."

—Fr. Wes Gristy, "More of the Story: A Guidebook for Our Season of Discernment," Lenten pastorates, 2019

How It Began

We had known for some time that we needed a new building. With the growth we were experiencing, we were quickly running out of room. Our nave was sometimes standing room only when we had special services, and we would have to bring in extra chairs. There was nowhere to store the extra chairs when they weren't being used, as our storage spaces were full of other furniture and materials. The choir vesting area, which was only about six feet square, doubled as a place to stack many of the extra chairs, so on Sunday mornings that space was crowded, to say the least, when choir members vested for the morning services. The kitchen, too, was often crowded, with the altar guild and hospitality team doing their best to share the limited counter and cabinet space. Our rooms for nursery and children's church were small and cramped for space as well.

In fall 2018, the Vestry introduced to the parish our vision of building a Mission Abbey. Architect Steve Carroll worked with the Vestry in designing a master site plan that addressed our vision. This was presented at the January 2019 Annual Parish Meeting.[1] In a letter addressed to All Saints, Fr. Wes outlined our progress:

> During Lent, we entered a season of discernment entitled 'More of the Story,' reflecting our desire to continue the story of All Saints in a way that is faithful to our beginnings. Over 120 people participated in one of our Lenten pastorates as we envisioned our life together on this piece of property and made financial commitments of over $1.4 million toward the construction of Phase 1, a new nave. And yet even before these funds were raised, the Vestry passed a resolution to set aside $75,000 over the next five years to be used toward our church planting efforts.[2]

On a very cold March 11, 2019, we shared a potluck meal at Nelson's Barn to learn more about our Mission Abbey project. Landon Preston gave us a "More of the Story" update on Mission Abbey and shared with us a video presentation that showed several members of the parish commenting on what we had experienced at All Saints. In that video, Jeff Garrety recalled that "it was never about the building. It was about relationships, of receiving Christ and following Him."[3]

There was a huge picture board on one wall with snapshots of All Saints parishioners and events from our past and present.

The Lenten pastorates in 2019 used a discernment guide

I Know the Plans I Have for You

Photo courtesy of All Saints Anglican Church

The Mission Abbey kickoff was held at Nelson's Barn, March 2019.

developed by Fr. Wes. This guide offered weekly opportunities for pastorates to recall the story of the early church, the story of All Saints, and to reflect on "More of the Story" of All Saints. In addition, each weekly meeting focused on a specific topic, which included discerning the Spirit's leading together, staying focused on the mission, being generous with our resources, and stepping out in faith.[4]

The commitment to develop our property was described as a strengthening in our parish life that "offers healing hospitality, nurtures family-like relationships, forms disciples in the Anglican way, eagerly serves others, and is financially generous and responsible."[5]

The first phase of this Mission Abbey would be the building of the nave. The Vestry formed four teams, each designed for a specific purpose. Landon Preston led the stewardship team, which included Rebecca Edgren, Jeff Garrety, Taylor Laird, Judy Rose, Shannon Stewart, Lloyd Tatum, and Jim Warmbrod. Donald Jordan chaired the communications team, which included members Jane Garrety, Kim Howerton, Caitlin Roach, Luke Sower, and David Thomas. Ben Mehr led the finance and accounting team, which had Rob Binkley, Vicki Burch, Bev Carr, and Lou Courcelle as members. Greg Jordan led the Phase I design team, which included Janet Brown, Leslie Creasy, David Laird, Joy Moore, and Sally Slack.[6]

Over the summer of 2019, our design team met with the architect and ministry groups from All Saints to finalize a design that would stay within our budget. A construction team was formed and a search for a general contractor was begun.

Ensuring that we stayed on the right track, we designed our fall pastorates to help us discern how the Holy Spirit might call each of us to use our talents in developing our vision.

In a letter addressed to All Saints parishioners, Fr. Wes reminded us that "building a building has never been our ultimate aim; it has been building the church, a community who 'shares in the life of God for the life of the world.' . . . We are not building a Mission Abbey so we can become something we have not already been, but so we can grow into more of what God has already created us to be."[7]

As Chris Pope commented in the Mission Abbey video, "One of the different things about this church is that next year always appears more exciting than this year."[8]

The Impact of COVID

By March 2020, we were finally planning to break ground for our new nave. Architectural plans had been finalized; we had received approval from the city of Jackson to proceed with the construction, arranged for financing, and hired Jeff Brasfield as our general contractor.

However, COVID intervened and forced us to re-evaluate the timing for breaking ground and to be wise stewards in anticipating how COVID would affect our budget. Thus, we entered a time of watching and waiting.[9]

Photo courtesy of Judy Rose

The procession for our breaking-ground service was held on October 10, 2021. Kevin Vailes and Fr. Ben Williams led the way.

In a letter to All Saints dated May 16, 2022, Stewardship Chair Landon Preston caught us up to date on Mission Abbey's progress since the onset of COVID. He reported that the concrete had been poured, the tower was being built, and the initial steel columns had been placed. He reported that over 90 percent of our families had made donations to build our new nave. As of May 16, 2022, about $1.7 million had been pledged toward Phase I of Mission Abbey, the nave. We had already secured a loan that would allow us to finish Phase I. The estimated cost to finish construction was $4 million at that time.[10]

Breaking Ground

On October 10, 2021, All Saints had a special outdoor service at the proposed site for our new nave.

Present were the architect, general contractor, site manager Bronson Doyle, and many All Saints parishioners. The service began with a procession into the area by our church family.

After proceeding to lawn chairs we had brought with us, we recited a brief "Bless the Build" litany with prayers, thanksgivings, intercessions, and Scripture readings.

We each received a bookmark and wildflower seeds to commemorate the occasion. A card attached to the flower seeds encouraged us to "enjoy this gift to celebrate what God has done and will do through All Saints." The bookmark reminded us to "pray for our church," and the wildflower seeds were given for us "to plant in faith of all that will come through Mission Abbey." Afterward, we enjoyed an outdoor meal together.

Over the months as the building began to take shape, we were excited as we came to church each Sunday to see how quickly things were happening.

Finally, the outside walls were built and covered with bricks and stone, a beautiful sight to see, but we could no longer see the progress that was taking place on the inside. We were just like children at Christmas, wanting to open our presents.

On a cold fall day in 2022, we were treated to a peek at what was going on inside the brick walls. We shared prayers and a brief liturgy and were asked to take markers and write on the studs things we felt led to share—Scripture, poems, songs, or other things that meant something to us. Eventually, these would all be covered over, of course, but we knew that we were building on a strong, spiritual foundation, both literally and figuratively.

Construction Site Accident

On June 3, 2022, Valentin Morales, one of the brick masons working on our nave, lost his footing on the scaffolding and fell about twenty feet to the ground.

Morales sustained several injuries, the most severe of them

Photos courtesy of Judy Rose

ABOVE: We had our first look at the inside of the new nave in November 2022.

LEFT: We began construction on the new nave in summer 2022.

being to his wrist. Fr. Wes was on sabbatical, so it fell to Fr. Ben Williams to oversee our church's initial response to Mr. Morales and his family.

According to the Vestry minutes dated June 14, 2022, contributions were made to the rector's discretionary fund and were distributed to the Morales family.[11]

CHAPTER TWELVE
Mission St. James

"Then Jesus came and spoke to them, saying, 'All authority has been given to Me in Heaven and on Earth. Go therefore and make disciples of all the nations, baptizing them in the name of the Father and of the Son and of the Holy Spirit.'"

—Matthew 28:18-19, NKJV

It Was There All Along

A look back at the earliest minutes of All Saints Board of Directors meetings in 2004 reveals that we were committed to church planting. This was not just an idea that appeared out of the blue a few years ago. Those early records of the board meetings all led with this reminder: Our goal as a board—keep the church-planting process moving along.

A Brief History

When All Saints decided that we needed a larger facility to accommodate our growth, it was also part of our plan to plant simultaneously another Anglican church in the area. Chris Pope, chair of the church-planting catalyst team, in an update on church planting at a parish forum on January 16, 2019, noted that All Saints is not trying to plant just one church; we are looking to be a parish that plants churches. The church-planting catalyst team has a vision of All Saints becoming a hub for Anglican churches throughout our region.[1]

In 2021, the Rev. Ben Williams joined our staff as curate in charge of church planting for a two-year season of discernment. He and his wife, Janie, and a few others started meeting in Kevin and Liz Vailes' home with unchurched people they invited to their fellowship. This reminds us of the early days of All Saints when we met in homes before finding a permanent place to worship. For a period of about three months before they formally launched, they met at the Water Tower at Lane College.

After many months of meeting in various locations, Mission St. James began meeting at Forest Heights United Methodist Church. On Sunday, April 16, 2023, during our regular morning services, All Saints blessed and sent out those who had become a part of Mission St. James. On April 23, Mission St. James had its official launch service. This began regular, weekly worship on Sunday afternoons at Forest Heights. Members of All Saints were encouraged to attend some of these services to show support for Mission St. James, and many of us attended at least one of them. Some members made the decision to become permanent members of our church plant.

CHAPTER THIRTEEN
Equipping for Ministry

"And He Himself gave some to be apostles, some prophets, some evangelists, and some pastors and teachers, for the equipping of the saints for the work of ministry, for the edifying of the body of Christ."
—Ephesians 4:11-12, NKJV

Ordained Ministry

Since becoming a church, All Saints has been blessed to witness the ordinations of several people to the diaconate and to the priesthood. Bob Hudson recalls he was told in September 2007 that Bishop Githiga would be ordaining him to the Holy Order of Deacons that next January. His ordination took place on January 5, 2008, at All Saints. At that time, the Rt. Rev. Bishop Bill Atwood was a bishop in the Anglican Church of Kenya and ordained Hudson for Bishop Githiga.

There was no national Anglican Church in America, so Hudson was ordained into the Anglican Church of Kenya. Hudson went on to earn a master of divinity degree from Trinity School for Ministry in Pennsylvania in May 2008 and assumed the duties of deacon in charge at St. Luke's Anglican Church in Maysville, Kentucky.[1]

Wes Gristy and Brian Larsen Wells were both ordained to the Sacred Order of Deacons in the ACNA on November 3, 2012, by Bishop Atwood.[2] Anticipating space constraints because of family members and friends of the two ordinands, plus members of All Saints who wished to attend, the ordination service was held at St. Mary's Catholic Church.

Just over a year later, on November 9, 2013, Fr. Wes and Fr. Brian were both ordained to the priesthood, again by Bishop Bill Atwood. This ordination service was also held at St. Mary's.[3] Fr. Wes became rector of All Saints in August 2014. Fr. Brian became priest to families in 2014; in 2021, he left the ordained ministry to enter medical school.

On October 31, 2015, Bishop Atwood ordained Ross Guthrie to the diaconate at All Saints.[4]

Deacon Guthrie completed a master's of Christian thought degree at Gordon-Conwell Theological Seminary in May 2016 and was ordained a priest in October 2016. He served as priest of spiritual formation at All Saints until leaving in 2019 to become the rector of Anglican Church of the Holy Trinity in North Augusta, South Carolina.[5]

Though not ordained at All Saints, Dr. Gary Osborne is an ordained minister and a licensed catechist in the parish ministry at All Saints. He was licensed by Bishop Atwood and then commissioned by Fr. Wes. A licensed catechist is one who teaches laity about the gospel of Jesus Christ. Emphasis is placed on the Anglican catechism.

Osborne has several master's degrees and a doctorate in counseling from Vanderbilt University. He has pastored several churches and is a volunteer chaplain at Jackson-Madison County General Hospital.

Osborne works part time in private practice, providing

Photos courtesy of All Saints Anglican Church and Judy Rose

Fr. Chuck Filiatreau, Fr. Brian Larson Wells, Fr. Ross Guthrie, Bishop Bill Atwood, and Fr. Wes Gristy, November 8, 2016.

LEFT: Deacons Nan Thomas and Terry Blakley. ABOVE RIGHT: Deacon Kevin Vailes. BOTTOM RIGHT: Deacon Barbara Reed.

counseling/psychotherapy in medical clinic settings.[6] He is a frequent pastorate leader at All Saints.

On October 30, 2021, Barbara Reed and Nancy Thomas were ordained to the vocational diaconate at All Saints by Bishop Bill Atwood.[7] Deacon Nan serves as minister of spiritual formation.

On June 3, 2023, Terry Blakley was ordained to the vocational diaconate, and Kevin Vailes was ordained as a transitional deacon by Bishop Atwood at All Saints. Kevin was appointed as the deacon of parish ministries at All Saints.

Serving Our Community

Several All Saints members have received special training to serve our community in unique ways. A list of services and those who provide them follows.

All Saints Immigration Services (ASIS)

Stacy Preston, executive director of ASIS, shared with me its history and how it became a US Department of Justice recognized organization in 2020.

ASIS had been a dream of Preston's. To see its birth in 2018 and its growth for the past five years has been a wonderful blessing for her. The accreditation followed a two-year, intense process that included forty hours of basic immigration law training. Preston and Dulce Maria Salcedo are both DOJ-accredited representatives, which means they can practice immigration law. ASIS has recently created a board of directors with Lynn Binkley as head of the board and Melinda Jordan as a member. The goal of ASIS is to keep families together. Its services are varied:

• ASIS representatives help clients renew their Deferred Action for Childhood Arrivals (DACA) status or screen for other eligible benefits.

• They help clients with first-time applications for green cards or renewal of green cards.

- They guide clients through the citizenship process.

Preston estimates that over 50 percent of ASIS clients are victims of domestic violence or immigrants from over thirty different countries.

ASIS sees only low-income clients, who pay for ASIS services on a sliding scale based upon their income. ASIS works with several other local agencies to get their clients the help they need. They rely on donations to provide all their legal services, since the fees clients pay do not cover these expenses.[8]

Grief Share

In 2019, after her experience with Grief Share at Second Presbyterian Church in Memphis following the death of her husband, Carrie Whaley went through leadership training to start a Grief Share ministry at All Saints. Second Presbyterian became a mentor to Carrie and her team—Paula Kirby, Rachel Strandquist, Donna Taylor, and Sheila Williamson—as they prepared to launch a Grief Share chapter at All Saints.

Due to COVID, they put their ministry on hold for a while, but eventually they were able to offer two Grief Share opportunities, one in the spring and another in the fall, in both 2020 and 2021. Grief Share is for anyone experiencing grief over the loss of a loved one. There are about ten sessions in each cycle of meetings. Grief Share continues to be offered at All Saints at least twice a year.[9]

Precept Bible Study

In 2019, Denise Matthews began to offer the precept Bible study for All Saints women and women throughout our community. She has been a precept leader for about ten years, so when she came to All Saints a few years ago, she continued that ministry. She said, "We study the Bible inductively, book by book. It's a fascinating way to study the Scriptures, 'precept upon precept,'" showing how Scripture ties into other Scripture.

Matthews's training included a three-day course in Chattanooga and mentoring for the first class she taught. She does continuing education on her own. In addition to the class she teaches in person, she also has internet classes, which reach a larger number of women from all over the world.

The classes vary in length, depending upon the length of the book of the Bible being studied. Matthews teaches her classes from home and extends her ministry to people in other parts of the United States and even in other countries via Zoom.[10]

CHAPTER FOURTEEN

To Everything There Is a Season

> "To everything there is a season,
> a time for every purpose under Heaven."
> —Ecclesiastes 3:1, NKJV

A New Diocese and a New Bishop

In 2022, Bishop Bill Atwood announced his plans to retire. He left the International Diocese two years later, in 2024. All Saints had been a part of that diocese since 2009, when the ACNA was formed. When Bishop Atwood's plans became known, he encouraged all the parishes in the International Diocese to go through a season of discernment in choosing whether to stay in the International Diocese or to join another diocese within the ACNA.

To that end, in January 2022, All Saints formed a diocesan discernment team, consisting of chairman Landon Preston, Jay Beavers, Marty Courcelle, Jane Garrety, Scott Huelin, and Lynn Tatum. They defined their goals as:

1. Mapping out the characteristics of a healthy diocese.
2. Assessing future diocesan options for All Saints.

3. Presenting their recommendation to the Vestry, with a Vestry decision expected by August 2023.

On April 30, 2023, the discernment team met with the membership of All Saints in a parish forum. They shared with us their work over the previous sixteen months and presented their findings. The following information is from the notes I took during that meeting.

The team did research on the eighteen Anglican dioceses in the United States. They used the characteristics of a healthy diocese they had identified in the beginning to narrow their search to two dioceses: the Anglican Diocese of the South (ADOTS), headed by Archbishop Foley Beach, and the Diocese of Christ Our Hope, led by Bishop Ordinary Steve Breedlove and Bishop Coadjutor Alan Hawkins. Team members conducted numerous interviews with these two dioceses.

The nine characteristics the discernment team looked for in a diocese are:

1. Canons who are responsible for tasks within the diocese.

2. A bishop who spends weekends with each church in turn, with a distinct process for ordination.

3. Systems for geographical focus on regions within the diocese.

4. Deaneries to carry feedback between churches and bishop.

5. Systems to support parishioners, such as youth, and to provide conferences for parishioners on prayer, culture, and more.

6. Making church planting a primary objective.

7. Theological robustness.

8. Systems to develop future generations of leadership/clergy.

9. Financial soundness and use of resources in specific ways. [1]

One thing particularly resonated with many who attended the forum. Our church plant, Mission St. James, was already a member of ADOTS, which meant that ADOTS was already involved in ministry in West Tennessee.

On September 24, 2023, Fr. Wes announced in church

that at its September 19, 2023, meeting, the Vestry had voted for the recommendation from the diocesan discernment team that All Saints become a part of ADOTS, with Archbishop Foley Beach, who is already our ACNA archbishop, becoming our diocesan bishop as well. This move became official in July 2024.

Archbishop Beach is a graduate of Georgia State University, the University of the South, and Gordon-Conwell Theological Seminary. Beach was elected archbishop of the ACNA in 2014.

Photo courtesy of All Saints

Fr. Bob Hudson and Archbishop Foley Beach on May 5, 2014.

In January 2018, Beach was elected by archbishops from around the world to chair the primates council of GAFCON.[2]

Bishop Atwood's June 2023 Visit

On June 3-4, 2023, Bishop Bill Atwood visited All Saints to ordain two new deacons, Terry Blakley and Kevin Vailes, and to confirm twelve new members into the Anglican Church. This would be his last visit in the old building.

One thing that made an impression on many of us was the sermon he preached on June 4. In that sermon, titled "Strength for the Call," Bishop Atwood challenged us as a church to get serious about our call as Christians.

"Jesus tells us to do something we have not done yet," he said. "We haven't taught all that He commands, we haven't baptized everybody, and we haven't made disciples of all nations. In fact, we haven't made disciples of this nation. . . . It's about time the Church steps up and fulfills our vocation that Jesus has given to us to disciple the land around us."[3]

In 1992, several things happened within the Episcopal Church that made it clear that they were turning away from God. Bishop Atwood was "anathematized by the national church headquarters and rejected from doing any teaching conferences or any consulting or anything else"[4] because of his stand to be obedient to the Lord. It was after reading in the church newspaper the presiding bishop's heretical Easter message that he asked God, "Now what do I do?"

"And, not out loud, but very, very clearly, the Lord spoke to me, and he said, 'Stop wasting time with leaders that are making the Church look like the world. Get on a plane and go to those places in the world where the bishops and archbishops are making the world around them look more like the Kingdom of God. Ask them for leadership and help.' And so I did . . ." Bishop Atwood continued. "Those of you involved in the early days of All Saints with Bishop Gideon Githiga from Thika coming, and after meeting him, many people said, 'Oooh, now I've seen a bishop!' "[5]

So eventually, All Saints and other like-minded churches became the Anglican Church in North America.

I asked Bishop Atwood what he would be doing, since he was retiring as bishop. He was already planning new projects.

"I will never retire," he said.[6] When Atwood left the International Diocese in 2024, he began assisting in the Anglican Diocese of the Southwest as well as continuing his work for Ekklesia, a non-profit he had founded years earlier.

Let us hope that Atwood doesn't retire and that he continues to be an outspoken voice for truth, as he was in his June 25, 2022, pastoral letter to churches in the diocese. In it, he addressed the Supreme Court decision overturning *Roe v. Wade*. Atwood outlined four responsibilities that we as Christians are called to do.

1. First, we are called to stand up and work to bring our states in line with the biblical principles of life. The decision to return abortion legislation to the states means that we need to pursue godly means to promote and respect life "from conception to natural death" where we can have the most impact.

2. Second, we are called to pray for pro-life leaders, especially the Supreme Court justices who ruled to overturn *Roe v. Wade*, churches, and ministries. Pray for their protection and efficacy. Look for ways we can support those who serve and their ministries.

3. Third, we must pray for those who are misled and have accepted and promote the abortion agenda, that God would open their eyes to understanding and grant them grace to repent and be obedient to Him.

4. Fourth, because God the Father has loved us before we even knew Him (1 John 4:19), we are called to discern how we can express His love in how we care for others. That is especially true in supporting pro-life and crisis pregnancy efforts. In the coming months, Bishop Atwood wrote, he would ask each congregation to discern and articulate their response to God's call to honor and respect life in this new environment.[7]

Leaving Our Old Building

On November 12, 2023, we attended our last Sunday morning worship services in our old building. It was a nostalgic time, especially for those who had been there since the beginning. Fr. Wes asked those who had been present that first Sunday, February 15, 2004, about twenty of us, to stand and be recognized, and we were each given a long-stemmed white rose. During the announcement time, David Laird shared some memories from those early days.

The choir sang in both services that Sunday, something we used to do every Sunday pre-COVID. Hymns included three that we had sung on February 15, 2004, our first Sunday in that building: "If Thou But Trust in God to Guide Thee," "Jesus, the Very Thought of Thee," and "A Mighty Fortress Is Our God."

It was only fitting that Fr. Chuck preached the last sermon from the old nave. And what a sermon it was! It challenged and motivated us to be the people God intended us to be and reminded us that we are defined, not by the building in which we worship, but by the people who worship in that building. Jane Garrety described it as "an incredible message that will transcend time."[8] She suggested that I include it in this book, and Linda Hayes and I totally agreed.

Fr. Chuck's Sermon: Blessed Is the Path Less Traveled

As Fr. Wes announced last week, this is the last Sunday we will be worshiping in this building, and he asked me to give the final homily. I don't know if that is because he needed a break or because I was the first rector when we first began worshiping in this building. In fact, he has chosen to use the exact same Scriptures that were used at the first service in this building as well as some of the same hymns.

When I was a child, there was a little saying we learned using our hands which you may remember. "This is the church. This is the steeple. Open the doors and see all the people."

At this point, Fr. Chuck put his hands together with his fingers entwined and folded against his palms. This represented the church building. The two index fingers were pointed up and touching at the tips to form a "steeple." When he opened his palms, his fingers became the "people" inside the church.

Yet when most people hear the word "church," they

immediately think of a building or place, not people. For instance, if I asked you to think about St. Mary's Catholic Church or First Methodist downtown or Love and Truth Church, most of you would immediately think of a building or place where they are located in the city, not the people who worship there.

When we read the Old Testament, we read in detail about the construction of the Temple, but what we mostly read about is people—Abraham, Isaac, Jacob, Moses, Joshua, David, Solomon, Isaiah, Jeremiah. When we read the New Testament, we read about the establishment of the early Church, but what we mostly read about is people—Nicodemus, Paul, John, Philemon, Timothy, Barnabas. And when we study Church history, even though there were magnificent edifices and cathedrals being built—the Cathedral of Saints Peter and Paul, Notre Dame, Westminster Abbey—what we mainly read about is people—Augustine, Aquinas, Martin Luther, Thomas Cranmer, Thomas Moore, John Wesley.

So also, though we have been blessed to be worshiping in this church building for almost twenty years, if you read a history of All Saints Anglican Church, and there is one currently being written, it is about people—Bishop Githiga, Bishop Atwood, Jeff Garrety, Joanie Forbes, Jordan Tang, Jim Warmbrod, Jake Stewart, the original founders, all the people baptized, confirmed, married, ordained, and buried from this place, or about the people like those in the Gospel reading who have experienced healing through the prayer ministry of All Saints, about Katie Beavers and the Catechesis of the Good Shepherd. The story of All Saints is a story about people led by the Holy Spirit, not this building which has served us so well.

In the Anglican Catechism, the question is asked: What is the Church? Answer: The Church is the whole community of faithful Christians in Heaven and on Earth, called and formed by God (not us) into one people.

The Church on Earth gathers to worship God in Word and

Sacrament, to serve God and neighbor, and to proclaim the Gospel to the ends of the earth.

One of the most well-known lines of poetry came from the pen of Robert Frost, in his poem "The Road Not Taken." He wrote: "Two roads diverged in a wood, and I—I took the one less traveled by, And that has made all the difference."

In 2004, a group of forty-plus families could go down the road their beloved Episcopal Church was following, or they could take a different road, one holding true to the Word of God as contained in Holy Scripture, one upholding orthodox faith and practice. They met and prayed, and they were led by the Holy Spirit to take that different road, and that has made all the difference: All Saints Anglican Church! It is all about people, orthodox people led by the Holy Spirit. As the people of All Saints move forward, we still need to remember even though we are now planted firmly in an orthodox diocese, advice and direction from the Church should be based solely on the Word of God. If it is not, it must be challenged. The Word of God is the final authority and unchangeable standard for the Christian faith and life.

That is why Psalm 1 is particularly appropriate for our last Sunday worshiping in this building and as a precursor to our move to the new nave next Sunday. Psalm 1 contrasts those who follow the law or teaching, and those who do not. It challenges us to make a choice between two distinct ways or roads. There is no third way.

Psalm 1 asks us to consider the path we take and challenges us to take the right path. There are no commands in Psalm 1. Yet it reads with the force of an exhortation that can be stated in three words: Choose God's way. In Matthew 7:13-14, Jesus says, "Enter by the narrow gate. For the gate is wide and the way is easy that leads to destruction, and those who enter it are many. For the gate is narrow and the way is hard that leads to life, and those who find it are few."

Notice that the first word of this psalm is the word "blessed," and the last word is "perish." What is the psalmist doing? He is taking us back to the whole motif of the Bible, to our first parents and the blessedness they knew under the shade of the Tree of Life, living life to the full. Then they rebelled and they ended up living amongst the thorns, perishing. The psalmist was saying to us in 2003 and he is saying to us in 2023, "Don't make their mistake!"

This is the message of Psalm 1. Choose God's way. What does it mean to choose God's way? It means to CHOOSE THE WAY THAT IS BLESSED. Blessed!

Interestingly, this is what Jesus called Peter in Matthew 16:17 after Peter confessed that Jesus was the Son of God and the Messiah, "Blessed are you, Simon Bar-Jonah! For flesh and blood has not revealed this to you, but by my Father who is in Heaven." It is also the way Jesus began His first recorded sermon in Matthew 5. We call these biblical "blessed are" statements beatitudes because in the Latin the word "blessed" is *beati*. That word "blessed" is *ashar* in Hebrew and *makarios* in Greek.

If you were to look up the meaning of the word "blessed" in a lexicon, it would say happy. But I think there is a good reason not to translate it as happy. Happy doesn't do this word justice. It doesn't have enough depth to it. For to be *ashar/makarios*—blessed—is to be happy as a result of receiving. *Ashar/makarios* is not just a feeling. It is a feeling that is produced by grace. This makes sense in light of how we tend to use it. If you were to ask me how I feel and I said happy, that would be different than if I said that I feel blessed. By saying blessed, I am saying I am happy, but that my happiness springs from something unmerited.

It's important to know that blessedness is not related to our circumstances. And it doesn't come simply by seeking for it. You find blessedness not by seeking it but by doing certain things and not doing other things. The blessing comes as a side benefit of the choices we make. We need to be clear on this: Blessings come not only from what we do, but also from what we don't do. Blessed people avoid certain things.

Psalm 1 surprises many people because it begins not with the positive but with a negative. The blessing begins with what the righteous person does not do.

He does not walk in the counsel of the wicked—meaning the advice of the morally unstable.

He does not stand in the way of sinners—which involves a series of lifestyle choices.

He does not sit in the seat of mockers, meaning to have close, intimate, long-term fellowship with those who reject the Word of God.

The psalmist starts with the negative but then moves to the positive side of the ledger. Having refused to walk in the way of evildoers, the blessed instead focus on knowing God's Word.

The blessed ones are those who delight in the law of the Lord. What is the law of the Lord? The word used here is actually *torah*, which is commonly used to refer to the first five books of the Old Testament, but *torah* in Hebrew means instruction. So, a good reading of this text is to say blessed are those who "delight in the instruction of the Lord"—which, of course, includes more than just the law, or the first five books of the Old Testament, but all of Scripture.

II Timothy 3:16 says, "All Scripture is breathed out by God and profitable for teaching, for reproof, for correction, and for training in righteousness, that the man of God may be complete, equipped for every good work."

Next week, worshiping in this place will be history. Time marches on. We have been blessed to have this building in which to worship for the past twenty years. Our desire, our hope, our prayer now, is to be blessed by God in our new nave.

Psalm 1 tells us how we can continue to be blessed in our new nave. This is God's prescription for blessedness, and what we discover is that blessedness relates to the way we live and the choices we make. It depends on the kind of people we are.

If we want to be blessed by God in our new nave, pay attention to this psalm.

"Blessed is the man who does not walk in the counsel of the wicked or stand in the way of sinners or sit in the seat of mockers. But his delight is in the law of the Lord, and on His law he meditates day and night. He is like a tree planted by streams of water, which yields its fruit in season and whose leaf does not wither. Whatever he does prospers." (Psalm 1:1-3)

Blessed is that man.

We are going to become like the people around us. This is true whether they are good or evil. So you avoid certain people and certain situations. Now as soon as I put it that way, I can imagine someone objecting. "But how are we going to reach the lost if we don't spend time with them?" Good question. The answer goes like this. You do not win the lost by living like the lost. You win the lost by loving the lost and living like the redeemed.

Our evangelical ancestors gave us the proper formula. They said we are to be "in the world but not of the world." That means we are to live among the lost, loving them, befriending them, caring for them, and at the same time, we are to live by an entirely different value system. We will not reach people by lowering our standards or compromising our values.

Blessedness will come by continuing to build the life of the community of people known as All Saints Anglican Church on the Word of God. This Word is as much needed at the beginning of this new season of life for All Saints as it was in 2004. If we desire God's blessing on this church, it is imperative to be mindful of the fact that the devil will oppose us at every turn.

The church (think people) that builds its life on the Word of God is like a tree planted by streams of water. The idea of a tree planted by streams of water speaks of a mighty tree with large branches and deep roots that go far down into the soil. Master gardeners, and there are about a dozen of them who are members of All Saints, will tell you that when you see a large tree that has been growing for many years, you can be certain that it has a vast, unseen root system. Many times, the root system will equal or exceed the part of the tree above ground. This is how the mighty sequoias last for centuries. Their unseen root systems give them stability against the changing forces of nature. In times of winter storms or summer drought, the roots hold the tree in place and ensure that it has enough moisture and nutrients to stay alive.

That's what a good root system will do for a church. How do you know when a tree has good roots? Answer: When the storms come. All the trees look pretty much alike when the sun is shining or a gentle rain is falling, but let a mighty storm with fierce rains and howling winds pass through. Then the true difference is apparent. The trees with few roots are blown over, but the trees with deep roots are still standing when the storm has passed. We, as a church, won't know how good our root system is until the storms of life crash against us. And be assured, they will.

The only way to be ready for the storm is for the whole church to be grounded in Scripture, continually building a foundation deep and strong for whatever may come our way. A church that is constantly refreshed by the Word of God, constantly renewed by the power of the Holy Spirit, never lives off yesterday's blessings, but lives each day in the strength of the Lord whose mercies are new every morning.

"This is the church, this is the steeple, open the doors and see all the people."

Going back to the Anglican Catechism: "What is the Church? The Church is the whole community of faithful Christians (people) in Heaven and on Earth, called and formed by God, not us, into one people. Because the Church is constituted by union with Jesus Christ, who is her head, that means that she is the only human community that transcends the boundary of death. At the end of history, Russia, China, the United States won't exist. Wall Street and the Supreme Court won't exist, and neither will this nave or the new nave we will worship in next Sunday, but God's people will. Think Romans 8:37 where in the midst of struggles, sorrow, persecution, famine, distress, nakedness, and the sword, those who know Jesus are "more than conquerors" through His divine power. And that triumphant delivery comes to us in large part through the Word of God.[9]

Delays

We had only two weeks' notice for when the actual move would take place. There had been several delays in getting last-minute things done, mainly paving the parking lot. Fr. Wes did not want to announce a move-in date until he had in hand something official from the city of Jackson allowing us occupancy. When the big announcement finally came, we had mere days to move all of the furnishings that would be needed for our first Sunday in the new nave. Those things couldn't be moved until we had worshiped for the last Sunday in the old nave.

Fr. Wes took advantage of having well-attended services that morning and asked that all able-bodied men remain afterward and help transport furniture and supplies that needed to be in the new building before the next Sunday.

Fr. Wes scheduled two workdays to finish the landscaping. He also announced a schedule for training sessions to be held during the upcoming week for ushers and greeters, nursery workers, sound techs, LEMs, and acolytes, as our new space would require new ways of doing things. The choir had its first training in the new nave that Tuesday, November 14.

Moving into Our New Building

When I pulled into the parking lot at nine in the morning on the day before our first service in the new nave, I saw that there was already a small crowd of parishioners performing last-minute jobs to ensure that we were ready for the day we had been eagerly anticipating for several months. There were gardeners working in the flower beds to finish the landscaping. Someone was hosing off the parking lot, while others were raking leaves. People were in the new kitchen preparing for our fellowship time the next day. Len Diffee and Dulce Maria Salcedo were busy vacuuming and cleaning. The altar guild was there to prepare the altar for the next day.

As previously mentioned, Denise Matthews used her extraordinary talents to make new linens for the altar. She also spent many hours researching, designing, and making the beautiful kneeler cushions at the altar rail. She and an advisory group made up of Fr. Chuck, Vicki Burch, and Kay Shearin came up with the final design based upon Fr. Chuck's brilliant idea to include symbols of the seven sacraments of the Anglican church.

With much pomp and circumstance, anticipation and excitement, and a feeling of awe at how God has blessed us, we moved into our new building on November 19, 2023, almost twenty years after we started worshiping together as the body of Christ on November 30, 2003.

The church was almost full, with 280 in attendance, including several visitors. It was a blessing that Walter Townsend, a member of our original Board of Directors of All Saints, and whose home was All Saints' first gathering place and where we decided we were a church, was able to come that day. Townsend gave the beautiful altar flowers in memory of his wife, Jane, and in honor of the All Saints founders and of Fr. Chuck. Jim and Halina Warmbrod drove from Nashville to be with us. Their home was one of the places we met before moving into the original building.

As a choral introit, the choir sang the familiar "Surely the Presence of the Lord," a hymn we had sung many times from our very beginning throughout our twenty-year history.

In his sermon that Sunday, Fr. Wes observed that it was fitting that this was the last day of our stewardship series and that the

Photo courtesy of Judy Rose

Our new nave, November 19, 2023.

Photo courtesy of Judy Rose

Mission Abbey, Phase I.

message of stewardship was exactly what we needed to hear on a day like that one. [10]

"We do not need to hear that this building is the result of any man's great ambition, or that this building is a monument of our collective ingenuity, or that this building somehow now legitimizes us as a church," Fr. Wes continued. "No, we need to be reminded once again that we are stewards of our time, and of our talents, and of our treasure—which is all certainly true. But we need to be reminded that we are primarily stewards of the very presence of God Himself. . . . This is what our new building is all about: a divine stewardship." [11]

Matthew Cook, parish administrator, had done a fantastic job of redesigning our Sunday bulletin, containing the announcements, upcoming events, and prayer lists so that we could do away with the inserts we once used. He also made attractive coordinating signs, which included our church logo, to identify various rooms in the building.

Moving into the new nave brought about some changes in our Sunday morning format. Since we would now be having only one worship service, a Christian formation hour was added before the main worship service, allowing all of us to partake in some kind of Christian formation. Adults would meet in the nave to learn more about Anglicanism, with possible topics being the Creeds and the Thirty-Nine Articles, and the study of various books of the Bible, and to participate in an in-depth instructed Eucharist. That first Sunday, Greg Jordan shared his thoughts on Philippians 4.

For the children, Christian formation would be in the original building, recently renamed the Parish Hall, and the children would continue to be taught the Catechesis of the Good Shepherd in a specially prepared environment called the Atrium.

Katie Beavers, lead children's catechist, wrote an article in the *Crown* to explain what the Atrium is. She recalled that in ancient times, it was a gathering place between the church and the street

I Know the Plans I Have for You

where those preparing for initiation into the church would be taught. Our Atrium would provide a similar space for our children as they learn to participate fully in the life of our parish. [12]

Deacon Kevin Vailes shared with me that the youth would also be meeting in the Parish Hall and would be involved in Christian formation that would help them learn more about our Anglican faith and practices. [13]

"God's Truth Abideth Still; His Kingdom Is Forever."
—"A Mighty Fortress," Martin Luther

So where should we go from here?

Now that we have this beautiful new building, do we become complacent and let the culture determine our agenda, or do we teach God's truth and leave our comfort zones and reach out to the lost and hurting in our community?

Do we follow the teaching of I Peter 3:15 "to be holy and set apart for the Lord God" and to "always be ready to tell everyone who asks you why you believe as you do"?

Bishop Atwood so aptly answered those questions for us in his June 4, 2023, sermon at All Saints. We would do well to remember his challenge to us:

"But we still have not done what Jesus told us to do—to teach all that He has commanded, to baptize in the name of the Father, Son, and Holy Spirit, and to disciple the nations. We need to ask what we need to do here in Jackson, Tennessee, to disciple this part of the world, and how do we manifest faithfulness to bring about the discipling of the whole nation and to participate in all the nations. How do we do that? We have to create a culture that says 'yes' to God and 'yes' to His Lordship, and, like Jesus, we go about our lives obeying what the Father is calling us to do. And we don't shrink back when it's costly." [14]

Let us remember our mission statement from 2003, "Empowered by the Holy Spirit, we will be disciples for Christ" and Fr. Wes's frequent reminder to us to "share in the life of God for the life of the world."

Rich Beitz said it well in the Mission Abbey video: "As long as the Vestry and the congregation continue to ask God where we're going and what we've got to do, and we follow His lead, I think this congregation will be fine." [15]

NOTES

Chapter 1: Storm Clouds Gathering

1. The *Jackson Sun*, May 6, 2003, vol. 155, issue 124, p. 1C.
2. The *Jackson Sun*, May 4, 2003, vol. 155, issue 122, p. 1B.
3. National Weather Service, Tornado Database, May 4, 2003, provided by Mark Rose, meteorologist, National Weather Service, Nashville, TN.
4. Frank T. Griswold, "A Statement from Presiding Bishop and Primate of the Episcopal Church, USA," August 6, 2003, www.episcopalchurch.org.
5. Frank T. Griswold, "The Presiding Bishop writes to the bishops before General Convention," June 13, 2003, www.episcopalchurch.org.
6. Lambeth Conference Archives, 1998, www.anglicancommunion.org.
7. Frank T. Griswold, "A Statement from Presiding Bishop and Primate of the Episcopal Church, USA," August 6, 2003, www.episcopalchurch.org.
8. Bob Hudson, email, June 30, 2022.
9. Charles Richards, conversation, June 6, 2022.
10. Op.cit.
11. Jeff Garrety, conversation, February 18, 2024.
12. Gretchen Filiatreau, handwritten notes, July 31, 2023.
13. Bob Hudson, email, June 30, 2022.
14. Fr. Charles Filiatreau, conversation, February 2023.
15. Op.cit.
16. Charles Richards, conversation, June 6, 2022.
17. "A Place to Stand: Declaring, Preparing," Episcopal.org/news: AAC Conference in Dallas, October 7-9, 2003.
18. Ibid.
19. Kathy Trawick, notes, 2003.
20. Op.cit.
21. Ibid.
22. David W. Virtue, "New Anglican Parish Forms in Jackson, Tennessee," Virtueonline.org, November 2004.
23. Lloyd Tatum, in-person conversation, May 7, 2023.

24. Fr. Charles Filiatreau, State of the Church, Annual Parish Meeting, St. Luke's Episcopal Church, December 7, 2003.
25. Walter Townsend, in-person conversation, June 3, 2022.

Chapter 2: Sheep Without a Shepherd
1. Kathy Trawick, notes, 2003.
2. Ibid.
3. Ibid.
4. Walter Townsend, in-person conversation, June 3, 2022.
5. Fr. Charles Filiatreau, in-person conversation, February 2023.
6. Kathy Trawick, notes, 2003.
7. Joanie Forbes, handwritten notes, January 16, 2023.
8. "More of the Story," Mission Abbey video, 2019.
9. Taylor Laird, telephone conversation, February 19, 2024.
10. Kathy Trawick, notes, 2003.
11. Joe Davis, telephone conversation, February 15, 2024.
12. Op.cit.
13. Taylor Laird, telephone conversation, February 15, 2024.
14. Charles Richards, in-person conversation, June 6, 2003.
15. Jane Garrety.
16. Kathy Trawick, notes, 2003.
17. Dr. Jim Warmbrod, email, March 4, 2023.
18. Fr. Charles Filiatreau, in-person conversation, February 2023.
19. Charles Richards, in-person conversation, June 6, 2022 .
20. Linda Hayes, in-person conversation, June 6, 2022.
21. Sally Slack, letter to Bishop Don Johnson, January 15, 2004.
22. David W. Virtue, "New Anglican Parish Forms in Jackson, Tennessee," Virtueonline.org, May 2004.
23. Ibid.
24. Ibid.
25. Ibid.
26. Ibid.
27. Bishop Don Johnson, "A Pastoral Letter from Bishop Johnson," www.episwtn.org, January 15, 2004.
28. Rev. Dr. Ephraim Radner, "A Response to Bishop Johnson's Letter,"

AAC News, January 16, 2004.
29. Bruce Mason, "Response to Bishop Johnson's 'Pastoral Letter,'" AAC News, January 16, 2004.

Chapter 3: Seek and Ye Shall Find

1. Bob Hudson, email, June 30, 2022.
2. "The First Bishop," Anglican Church of Kenya, Thika Diocese website; December 18, 2006, p. 1.
3. Jeff Garrety, journal entry, August 24, 2007.
4. Bishop Gideon Githiga, sermon at All Saints Anglican Church, June 27, 2004.
5. Jeff Garrety, letter to Bishop Gideon Githiga, February 10, 2004.
6. Jeff Garrety, journal entry, August 24, 2007.
7. Gretchen Filiatreau, handwritten notes, July 31, 2023.
8. Kathy Trawick, notes, 2004.
9. Ibid.
10. Op.cit.
11. Sunday bulletin, All Saints Anglican Church, June 27, 2004.
12. Bishop Gideon Githiga, sermon at All Saints Anglican Church, June 27, 2004.
13. Bishop Gideon Githiga, "There Is Great Hope for Episcopalians!" The American Anglican Council Midsouth Chapter, July 4, 2004.
14. Gretchen Filiatreau, handwritten notes, July 31, 2023.
15. Ibid.
16. Ibid.
17. Vestry minutes, August 9, 2004.
18. Pastoral letter, Bishop Don Johnson, August 3, 2004.
19. Walter Townsend, in-person conversation, June 3, 2022.
20. Joanie Forbes, handwritten notes, January 16, 2023.
21. Kathy Trawick, notes, November 30, 2003.
22. Op.cit.
23. Ibid.
24. Ibid.
25. Sunday bulletin, All Saints Anglican Church, February 15, 2004.
26. "All Saints Anglican Church Welcomes Fr. Charles Filiatreau,"

the *Crown*, volume 1, issue 7, September, 2004, p. 2.
27. Fr. Charles Filiatreau, letter to the Parish of St. Luke's Episcopal Church, May 3, 2004.
28. Preston Atkinson, Letters to the Editor, the *Jackson Sun*, May 11, 2004, vol. 155, issue 129.
29. Fr. Chuck Filiatreau, in-person conversation, February 2023.
30. Kathy Trawick, notes, 2004.
31. Jane Garrety, search committee meeting on March 17, 2004 (email sent to board members on March 18, 2004).
32. Joe Davis, telephone conversation, February 15, 2024.
33. Walter Townsend, in-person conversation, June 3, 2022.
34. Fr. Charles Filiatreau, in-person conversation, February 2023.
35. Joanie Forbes, handwritten notes, January 16, 2023.
36. Fr. Charles and Gretchen Filiatreau, "To the members of All Saints," the *Crown*, July 2004, vol. 1, issue 5, p. 3.

Chapter 4: The Lord Works in Mysterious Ways
1. Gretchen Filiatreau, handwritten notes, July 31, 2023.
2. Marty Courcelle, in-person conversation, August 27, 2023.
3. Op.cit.

Chapter 5: Our Kenyan Connection
1. Gretchen Filiatreau, handwritten notes, July 31, 2023.
2. Fr. Charles Filiatreau, email to Bishop Gideon Githiga, January 8, 2007.
3. Dr. Jordan Tang, in-person conversation, August 31, 2023.
4. Gretchen Filiatreau, handwritten notes, July 31, 2023.
5. Ibid.
6. Jeff Garrety, journal entry, April 15, 2005.
7. Jeff Garrety, journal entry, August 24, 2013.

Chapter 6: The Move
1. Anne Rushing, in-person conversation, March 5, 2023.
2. The *Crown*, volume 4, issue 6, September 2006, p. 3.
3. Joanie Forbes, handwritten notes, January 16, 2023.

4. The *Crown*, volume 2, issue 2, February 2005, p. 3.
5. Vestry minutes, December 6, 2004.
6. Bill Boggs, report to Annual Parish Meeting, December 12, 2004.
7. The *Crown*, volume 2, issue 4, p. 6, April 2005.
8. Gretchen Filiatreau, handwritten notes, July 31, 2023.
9. Ibid.

Chapter 7: Decently and in Order

1. Joanie Forbes, handwritten notes, January 16, 2023.
2. Sunday bulletin, All Saints Anglican Church, June 20, 2004.
3. Sunday bulletin, All Saints Anglican Church, June 27, 2004
4. The *Crown*, volume 1, issue 5, July 2004, p. 3.
5. Vestry minutes, All Saints Anglican Church, December 6, 2004.
6. Membership Expectations, All Saints Anglican Church, September 23, 2004.
7. Ibid.
8. "Rooted Growth," 2016 Annual Report, All Saints Anglican Church.
9. Kathy Trawick, "A Learning Experience," church newsletter, p. 2, March 2004, vol. 1, issue 2.
10. The *Crown*, volume 3, issue 8, September 2005, p. 4.
11. Gretchen Filiatreau, handwritten notes, July 31, 2023.
12. Ibid.

Chapter 8: Disciples for Christ

1. Kathy Trawick, notes, 2004.
2. Jane Garrety, report to the Annual Parish Meeting, December 12, 2004, pp. 12-13.
3. Joanna Priester, telephone conversation, January 5, 2024.
4. Ibid.
5. "Youth Christian Education" report, All Saints Anglican Church (unnamed author), January 25, 2004.
6. Courtney Davison, report to Annual Parish Meeting, December 12, 2004, p. 5.
7. The *Crown*, volume 2, issue 6, June 2005, p. 1.

8. The *Crown*, volume 4, issue 7, July 2007, p. 5.
9. Anne Rushing, in-person conversation, March 5, 2023.
10. Ibid.
11. The *Crown*, volume 7, issue 4, April 2009, p. 6.
12. The *Crown*, volume 8, issue 2, February 2010, p. 6.
13. The *Crown*, volume 7, issue 3, March 2009, p.5.
14. The *Crown*, volume 3, issue 10, November 2005, p. 1.
15. Melinda Pearson, telephone conversation, May 16, 2023.
16. The *Crown*, volume 9, issue 7, July 2011, p.1.
17. Op.cit.
18. Taylor Laird, report to Annual Parish Meeting, December 12, 2004, p. 5.
19. Kathy Herriman, notes, 2004.
20. Lloyd Tatum, newsletter, All Saints Anglican Church, March 2004, volume 1, issue 1.
21. Jane Garrety, in-person conversation, February 8, 2024.
22. Kathy Herriman, notes, 2004.
23. Jim Warmbrod, report to Annual Parish Meeting, December 12, 2004.
24. Gretchen Filiatreau, handwritten notes, July 31, 2004.
25. Linda Davenport, report to Annual Parish Meeting, December 12, 2004, pp. 9-11.
26. Gretchen Filiatreau, conversation, August 20, 2023.
27. Op.cit.
28. Julie Cook, 101.5 FM NEWS/TALK WNWS, May 17, 2023.
29. Kathy Trawick, notes, 2004.
30. Gretchen Filiatreau, handwritten notes, July 31, 2023.

Chapter 9: Caring for Our Church Family
1. Terry Blakley, in-person conversation, February 23, 2024.
2. Terry Blakley, email, March 17, 2024.
3. Op.cit.
4. Terry Blakley, in-person conversation, March 1, 2024.
5. Ibid.
6. Terry Blakley, email, March 17, 2024.

7. Nan Thomas, "Choosing Solitude & Silence," the *Crown*, September 2003, p. 7.
8. Linda Hayes, report to Annual Parish Meeting, December 12, 2004, pp. 7-8.
9. Celeste Pope, in-person conversation, January 7, 2024.
10. Joanie Forbes, handwritten notes, January 16, 2023.
11. Gretchen Filiatreau, handwritten notes, July 31, 2023.
12. Joanie Forbes, report to Annual Parish Meeting, December 12, 2004, pp. 6-7.
13. Ibid.
14. Gretchen Filiatreau, handwritten notes, July 31, 2023.
15. Joanie Forbes, handwritten notes, January 16, 2023.
16. Bev Carr, telephone conversation, October 27, 2023.
17. Dr. Jordan Tang, in-person conversation, August 31, 2023.
18. Gretchen Filiatreau, handwritten notes, July 31, 2023.
19. Op.cit.
20. Ibid.
21. Becky Googe, telephone conversation, October 3, 2023.
22. Becky Googe, report to Annual Parish Meeting, January 13, 2008, p. 5.
23. Ibid.
24. Marty Courcelle, in-person conversation, August 27, 2023.
25. Denise Matthews, in-person conversation, Fall 2023.
26. Sally Slack, in-person conversation, February 25, 2024.
27. John Herriman, report to Annual Parish Meeting, December 12, 2004, pp. 8-9.
28. Charles Richards, report to Annual Parish Meeting, December 12, 2004, p. 8.

Chapter 10: Rejoice in the Lord Always

1. Gretchen Filiatreau, handwritten notes, July 31, 2023.
2. Ibid.
3. The *Crown*, volume 1, issue 7, September 2004, p. 3.
4. The *Crown*, volume 4, issue 3, May 2006, p. 7.
5. Ibid., p. 2.
6. Parish Registry, All Saints Anglican Church.

7. Ibid.
8. Bishop Bill Atwood's biographical information, International Diocese website, idio.net.
9. *The Way, the Truth, and the Life: Theological Resources for a Pilgrimage to a Global Anglican Future*, May 2008, p. 5.
10. Ibid., p. 5.
11. Ibid., p. 6.
12. Ibid., pp. 21-28.
13. Jeff Garrety, written comments on GAFCON, May 2008.
14. "Pilgrim's Progress," GAFCON Jerusalem 2008, Tuesday, June 23, 2008.
15. "Resolution of All Saints Anglican Church to affiliate with the International Diocese of the Anglican Church in North America," the *Crown*, volume 7, issue 4, April 2009, p. 3.
16. Gretchen Filiatreau, handwritten notes, July 31, 2023.
17. Ibid.
18. Ibid.
19. Ibid.
20. Fr. Wes Gristy, in-person conversation, August 23, 2022.
21. Wes and Abbie Gristy, "The Appeal of Anglicanism," Summer 2012.
22. Fr. Wes Gristy, in-person conversation, February 13, 2024.
23. Service bulletin, "The Ordination of Wesley Adam Gristy and Brian Patrick Larsen Wells to the Sacred Order of Deacons," November 3, 2012.
24. Service bulletin, "The Ordination of The Reverend Wesley Adam Gristy and The Reverend Brian Patrick Larsen Wells to the Sacred Order of Priests," November 9, 2013.
25. Service bulletin, "The Installation of the Reverend Wesley Adam Gristy as the Rector of All Saints Anglican Church," August 24, 2014.
26. Sunday bulletin, All Saints Anglican Church February 17, 2019.
27. The *Crown*, volume 8, issue 3, March 2010, p. 2.
28. The *Crown*, volume 8, issue 2, February 2010, p. 1.

Chapter 11: Mission Abbey

1. Annual Parish Meeting, January 2019.

I Know the Plans I Have for You 153

2. Fr. Wes Gristy, letter addressed to All Saints, September 19, 2019.
3. "More of the Story," Mission Abbey video, 2019.
4. Fr. Wes Gristy, "More of the Story—Building a Mission Abbey, A Guidebook for Our Season of Discernment," Lenten pastorates, 2019.
5. The *Crown*, February 2009.
6. Ibid.
7. Fr. Wes Gristy, letter addressed to All Saints, May 18, 2020.
8. "More of the Story," Mission Abbey video, 2019.
9. Op.cit.
10. Landon Preston, letter to All Saints, May 16, 2022.
11. Kay Shearin, email, March 28, 2023.

Chapter 12: Mission St. James

1. Chris Pope, update on church planting, parish forum, January 16, 2019.

Chapter 13: Equipping for Ministry

1. Bob Hudson, email, April 2023.
2. Service bulletin for "The Ordination of Wesley Adam Gristy and Brian Patrick Larsen Wells to the Sacred Order of Deacons," November 3, 2012.
3. Service bulletin for "The Ordination of The Reverend Wesley Adam Gristy and The Reverend Brian Patrick Larsen Wells to the Sacred Order of Priests," November 9, 2013.
4. Service bulletin for "The Ordination of Ross Daniel Guthrie to the Sacred Order of Deacons," October 31, 2015.
5. Anglican Church of the Holy Trinity, North Augusta, South Carolina, website, March 31, 2023.
6. Gary Osborne, email, April 1, 2024.
7. Service bulletin for "The Ordination of Barbara Reed and Nancy Thomas to the Sacred Order of Deacons," October 30, 2021.
8. Stacy Preston, in-person conversation, May 25, 2023.
9. Carrie Whaley, telephone conversation, May 3, 2023.
10. Denise Matthews, telephone conversation, September 7, 2023.

Chapter 14: To Everything There Is a Season

1. Parish forum, All Saints Anglican Church, April 30, 2023.
2. Archbishop Foley Beach biography, AnglicanChurch.net.
3. Bishop Bill Atwood, "Strength for the Call," sermon at All Saints Anglican Church, June 4, 2023.
4. Ibid.
5. Ibid.
6. Conversation with Bishop Bill Atwood, June 3, 2023.
7. Bishop Bill Atwood, "A Pastoral Letter for the International Diocese," June 25, 2022.
8. Jane Garrety, email, November 12, 2023.
9. Fr. Charles Filiatreau, "Blessed Is the Path Less Traveled," sermon at All Saints Anglican Church, November 12, 2023.
10. Fr. Wes Gristy, "Faithful Stewards of God's Presence," sermon at All Saints Anglican Church, November 19, 2003.
11. Ibid.
12. Katie Beavers, "All About the Atrium," the *Crown*, September 2023.
13. Conversation with Kevin Vailes, November 2, 2023.
14. Bishop Bill Atwood, "Strength for the Call," sermon at All Saints Anglican Church, June 4, 2023.
15. "More of the Story," Mission Abbey video, 2019.

APPENDIX

Founding Members of All Saints

The following are the founding members who were present for the signing of a document outlining our purpose and mission on February 15, 2004. A few others were present but did not sign.

Caroline Bagley	Jeff Ham	Joanna Priester
Jim Bagley	Rezina Ham	Charles Richards
Bill Boggs	Nelda Harrison	William Richards
Lou Courcelle	Linda Hayes	Judy Rose
Marty Courcelle	Tom Hayes	Anne Rushing
Carolyn Crowell	John Herriman	Duane Rushing
Linda Davenport	Kathy Herriman	Don Sprinkle
Joe Davis	Andy Hudson	Harmony Sprinkle
Rita Davis	Barbara Hudson	Lloyd Tatum
Courtncy Davison	Robert Hudson	Jane Townsend
Catherine Falk	David Laird	Walter Townsend
David Falk	Taylor Laird	Debbi Wagner
Joanie Forbes	Robert McDermid	Rich Wagner
Jane Garrety	Malcolm Pearson	Dennis Ward
Jeff Garrety	Melinda Pearson	Mary Ward
Becky Googe	Bob Phillips	Jim Warmbrod
Wendy Googe	Shirley Phillips	Halina Warmbrod
Roseanne Grimball	Brad Priester	

All Saints Stewards/Board of Directors
Jane Garrety
Robert Hudson
Lloyd Tatum
Walter Townsend

Initial Ministry Chairs
(before our first Vestry was formed)
Altar guild—Marty Courcelle
Acolyte master—Jim Bagley
Chalice bearers—Jim Bagley
Choir—Joanie Forbes
Christian education—Taylor Laird
Facilities—Bill Boggs
New members—John Herriman
Newsletter—Kathy Herriman
Nursery—Harmony Sprinkle
Pastoral care—Judy Rose
Pastoral care assistant—Rosie Grimball
Stewardship—Jim Warmbrod
Youth choir—Becky Googe

All Saints Music Directors
Joanie Forbes, 2004-2008
Becky Googe, choristers, 2006-2008
Bev Carr, 2008-2009
Dr. Randall Bush, 2009-2013
Dr. Jordan Tang, 2013-present

All Saints Clergy

- **The Right Reverend Gideon G. Githiga**—bishop of the Diocese of Thika, Kenya, 2004-2010
- **The Right Reverend Benjamin Nzimbi**—archbishop of the Province of Kenya, 2004-2010
- **The Right Reverend Dr. Bill Atwood**—bishop of the International Diocese in the Anglican Church of North America, 2010-2024
- **Archbishop Foley Beach**—bishop of the Anglican Diocese of the South and archbishop of the Anglican Church of North America, 2010-present. Beach will also become our bishop when our affiliation with ADOTS becomes official in July 2024.
- **The Reverend Charles L. Filiatreau**—rector, 2004-2015; rector emeritus, 2015-present
- **The Reverend Justin Baldwin**—associate priest to youth, 2009-2010
- **The Reverend Wes Gristy**—associate pastor for programs, 2013; co-rector, 2014; rector, 2015-present
- **The Reverend Brian Larsen Wells**—associate pastor to youth, 2013-2014; priest to families, 2014-2021
- **The Reverend Ross Guthrie**—pastor/priest of spiritual formation, 2016-2020
- **The Reverend Ben Williams**—curate for church planting, 2021-2023
- **The Reverend Dr. Gary Osborne**—licensed catechist, 2013-present
- **Deacon Barbara Reed**—2022-present
- **Deacon Nancy Thomas**—2022-present
- **Deacon Terry Blakley**—2023-present
- **Deacon Kevin Vailes**—2023-present

All Saints First Vestry and Ministry Chairs

VESTRY
Bill Boggs
Linda Davenport
Jeff Garrety, rector's warden
Tom Hayes, treasurer
John Herriman
Bob Hudson, people's warden
Taylor Laird
Judy Rose, clerk
Debbi Wagner
Jim Warmbrod

MINISTRY CHAIRS
Altar guild—Marty Courcelle
Acolyte master—Jim Bagley
Buildings and grounds—Bill Boggs
Choir—Joanie Forbes
Christian formation—Taylor Laird
Hospitality/fellowship—Linda Hayes
Hospitality/fellowship assistant—Joanna Priester
Lay Eucharistic ministers—Jim Bagley
Lectors—Charles Richards
New members—John Herriman
Newsletter—Kathy Herriman
Nursery—Harmony Sprinkle
Outreach—Linda Davenport
Pastoral care—Judy Rose
Pastoral care assistant—Rosie Grimball
Stewardship—Jim Warmbrod
Youth choir—Becky Googe

Gifts to All Saints

A Little Background

These comments and the lists that follow are from Gretchen Filiatreau's handwritten notes, July 31, 2023.

"It is no small task to outfit an Anglican altar. The symbolic concept is taken from the Tabernacle of God's design in the wilderness. Everything behind the communion rail represents the Holy of Holies where the Lord Himself could be encountered. For this reason, any remaining blessed bread from Holy Communion is locked in the ambry. Blessed wine is consumed right then. The wine is mixed with water to symbolize the water and blood, which flowed when Christ was pierced in His side on the cross. Any remaining liquid in the altar pieces or from washing is poured out on the ground rather than being drained into an unclean sewer.

"Because Christ is Holy, we offer Him our very best. The fair linen and purificators from the altar are kept meticulously clean by members of the altar guild. This is why only fresh flowers and fresh foliage are offered on the altar.

"Our very first 'altar' was the table that now stands at the center aisle at the back of the church. It was covered by a beautiful antique lace and linen cloth given by the late Catherine Falk. The silver candlesticks (the ones we had then) were loaned by Jane and Walter Townsend. The Filiatreaus loaned their hand-painted Peruvian bookstand for the service book. Fr. Chuck said he thought a pottery chalice and paten had been loaned by Noland Pipes. It was a picture of lovely simplicity."

Original Altar Furnishings

1. Antique wine decanters of silver and crystal, purchased in England, were given by Fr. Chuck and Gretchen Filiatreau; the crystal was broken accidentally.

2. A silver piece was given by Liz Wallis and family as a memorial

for her mother, Betty Butler, an early member of All Saints; it leaked periodically. The silversmith said it could not be repaired again.

3. Our current flagon was purchased by the church and found by Fr. Chuck at the Silver Vaults in London, England.

Other Gifts

1. The wooden cross behind the altar was given by Virginia Cox in honor of Jane and Walter Townsend and was removed to the new nave in mid-2023.

2. The original altar was given by Lupe Mitchell as a memorial to her daughter, Prissy Maness. It is now located in the hospitality area in the new nave.

3. A pair of silver altar candles, a bread box, and a lavabo were given by Brad and Angie Box in honor of their children Weston, Jenna, Marshall, and Jondavid.

4. A chalice and paten, made in Spain, were given by Walter Townsend in memory of his wife, Jane.

5. A second chalice was given by Grace Ann House and Brad and Angie Box.

6. A service book was given by an unknown donor.

7. An altar bookstand for the service book was given by Brad and Joanna Priester in honor of Fr. Chuck.

8. A ciborium was given by Lou and Marty Courcelle.

9. Two silver cruets were given by Carlin Diffee.

10. The processional cross was given by Rich and Debbi Wagner as a memorial to their son Matthew.

11. The original ambry was made by Kenny Hanson. It and the ambry candle were donated by Bob and Barbara Hudson.

12. The baptismal ewer was donated by Jim and Halina Warmbrod.

13. A pair of silver trumpet vases for altar flowers was given by Jane Townsend in honor of Walter Townsend.

14. A pair of processional candles was given by Fr. Chuck

and Gretchen Filiatreau as a memorial to her uncle, Vincent Voorhees Lane.

15. A lectern was given by Fr. Chuck and Gretchen Filiatreau. Gretchen purchased this at a used furniture store just before their wedding, thinking, "Chuck might need a pulpit of his own someday." It was a bookstand at home for the family Bible.

16. Two alms basins were given by Jane and Walter Townsend. Two others were given by Walter in memory of Addison Stone.

17. The children's cross, maybe a church purchase, was added at Fr. Chuck's suggestion as a guide for the children to keep them from dashing out to children's church after the children's sermon.

18. The All Saints banner was designed by Debbi Wagner and Joanie Forbes and was handmade by Joanie Forbes.

19. The votive candle stand was made by Kenny Hanson and given by Kenny and Sarah Beth in memory of her mother.

20. The Steinway baby grand piano was given by Harris Lake Smith, bequeathed to us in his will.

21. Chime bars were given by Bob and Barbara Hudson.

Gifts Elsewhere in the Church

1. The original cross was given by the founders.

2. The sign we see as we exit the driveway, "You are now entering the mission field," was given by Jeff and Jane Garrety.

3. An antique desk and office chair were given by Sally Dabney. They were used by Fr. Chuck until his retirement. Afterward, they were moved to the office adjacent to the church office.

4. Fr. Chuck's picture, purchased by the church, now hangs on the wall at the main entrance to the new nave.

5. A complete set of dishes was procured by Shirley Phillips and bought by the church.

6. The antique church pew in the back of the old nave was given by Jim and Halina Warmbrod and came from a church Jim attended as a child. This pew is now in the hospitality area of the new nave.

7. A sideboard, bookcase, china cabinet, dining room table and chairs, and two plant stands were given by Jim and Halina Warmbrod when they moved to Nashville in 2020.

Altar Furnishings and Other Gifts Given for the New Nave

1. An ambry, which holds blessed elements, was made by Ben Matthews. (This replaces the original ambry and candle donated by Bob and Barbara Hudson.)

2. Padded kneelers for the altar, along with various altar linens, were made and donated by Denise Matthews.

Judy Rose is a retired teacher who volunteers at a pro-life pregnancy clinic near her home in Jackson, Tennessee. She sings in the choir and serves on the altar guild at All Saints. Her family includes two sons, their wives, and a grandson.

All Saints Anglican Church members Linda Hayes and Jane Garrety assisted Rose in producing this book.